LIFTED BY LOVE

LESSONS FROM THE LIFE OF PETER

Patricia Clarke

WESTBOW
P R E S S®
A DIVISION OF THOMAS NELSON
& ZONDERVAN

WestBow Press books may be ordered through booksellers or by contacting:

WestBow Press
A Division of Thomas Nelson & Zondervan
1663 Liberty Drive
Bloomington, IN 47403
www.westbowpress.com
844-714-3454

ISBN: 978-1-6642-6758-9 (sc)
ISBN: 978-1-6642-6757-2 (e)

Print information available on the last page.

WestBow Press rev. date: 07/07/2022

CONTENTS

ACKNOWLEDGMENTS

The idea for *Lifted by Love: Lessons from the Life of Peter* began years ago while teaching at a retreat, but it took many people for this Bible study to make it into the world. Thank you to Amy Julia Becker, Nan Clarke, Emily Dubose, Kim Greene, Susan Girone Higgins, Mary Brooks Jamison, Virginia Syer, Weezie Thompson, and Tommy Thompson for your encouragement, editing, input, and contributions to this project.

INTRODUCTION

Hello, and welcome! My name is Patricia Clarke, and it is an honor to guide you as we study the life of Peter together. In the following weeks, I hope Peter will emerge not as a deceased saint or an influential man in history, but as a human we can relate to with regular aspirations and limitations. Sometimes Peter is brave and bold, and other times he is foolish and cowardly. Like many of us, he has belief and doubt, faith and fear. He shows devotion one moment and betrayal the next. But in spite of Peter's inconsistent nature and frustrating flaws, Jesus befriends him, teaches him, and calls him by name to follow Him.

When I started studying the life of Peter, one story captivated me in particular—the account of Jesus calling Peter to get out of his fishing boat, step onto the water, and walk toward Him. What piqued my interest is that Peter asks to get out of the boat. Why does he do this? Why does Peter *want* to leave his tried-and-true vessel, the place that he's learned to rely on in the middle of a storm? Why not stay on board and play it safe? In what way is this a metaphor for all of us at some point in our adult lives?

At this time in the events of Peter's life, he is at a crossroads. His boat provides security, and since he is a professional fisherman, it is how he makes a living. But once he meets Jesus, the boat he uses to navigate the waters of his life—the life that is familiar and comfortable, the one that represents his old way of living—no longer fits him. To leave that boat-life and follow Jesus, he puts everything he depends on at risk. Physically stepping out of the boat symbolizes the decision he is about to make with the direction of his life. If Jesus is not the Messiah, if there is no Divine Power, then stepping out of the boat is foolish. If He is, then returning to his old way of life is also foolish. It is either one or the other. Peter must answer the question for himself, but can he do that if he stays inside the boat? Purposeful risk, in response to God's call, activates faith. When Peter's foot hits the water, like a defibrillator to the heart, his faith, grown feeble from years of waiting for the Messiah, wakes up.

When Peter entrusts his life to Jesus, Peter becomes His disciple, following His ways like an apprentice. Peter walks with Jesus, he watches Jesus, and he learns a new approach to living. Jesus's radical teaching on love, His upside-down way of viewing power structures, His servant style of leadership, and His ultimate demonstration of sacrifice lift Peter from being an ordinary person to being an extraordinary founder of a community based on values the world had never seen before. Peter finds a new spirit growing within him, one that is at once his own spirit—fully human—and yet enlivened, awakened, and emboldened by the Spirit of God. As we study Peter's life together, that same Spirit invites us to join Peter in this new way of living, a way that is lifted by love.

This love is not a sugary, pink heart emoji love, or a sentimental, ungrounded-in-the-grit-of-life love, but rather a revolutionary, efficacious love that changes all that has been and all that will be. Far from a fleeting emotion, Jesus's love changes Peter in concrete and lasting ways. In each week's study, we discuss one of the following questions as it pertains, not only to Peter, but to us as well: Who is in charge? What do I want? Who do I trust? Am I good enough? What is love? What is grace? Who am I? And where am I going? In doing so, we explore the core essentials of the gospel, which is the good news of God's love for humanity in Jesus Christ.

The story of Peter walking on water serves as a template for so many moments in our lives. Whether it's a pivotol moment—when a person struggling with addiction surrenders to a higher power—or a hidden moment—when a woman's life is unraveling and she whispers a simple prayer for help—following Jesus means accepting that our old way of life isn't working and we don't know how to fix it. It means leaving a self-centric way behind. Following Jesus means letting His limitless love live in us, sustain us, and extend through us to others. Practically speaking, what does that look like? The Weekend Reflection Questions, the readings, the podcasts, and the group conversations will explore this question. Each component of the study, in its own unique way, plays a vital role in our understanding and application of a more loving life. For the most impact, I encourage you to engage with this study on both a personal and community level, taking time alone *and* with a group to process the material. When we step out of the boat, we falter, fall, and sink; but like He did for Peter, Jesus will stretch out His hand to steady us and lift us up. The stepping is ours to do; the lifting is His. Let's get started!

GUIDELINES FOR THE WEEKEND READING AND REFLECTION QUESTIONS

1. On the weekend before your group meets, find some time to relax, read, and reflect on the questions for the week. Make this time enjoyable! Pour a mug of coffee or light a candle and get comfortable in your favorite chair. This time is for you to recharge. For this section, you will need a Bible and a pen. The Bible translations I use are the New International Version (NIV), the New Revised Standard Version (NRSV), the English Standard Version (ESV), and the Literal Standard Version (LSV). I particularly recommend *The Life with God Bible* for the NRSV.

2. Depending on the lesson and the pace you prefer, the **Weekend Reading and Reflection** questions take about thirty minutes. Feel free to spread these out over a couple of days, or complete them in one sitting.

3. The answers come directly from the text. They don't require any previous knowledge of the Bible. Think of each lesson as a meal. Just as chewing enables us to eat food, *writing* key phrases from the text, *answering* simple questions, and then *discussing* the content allow us to digest the material and incorporate it into our lives. If we only think about what we read and never speak or write about it, we don't absorb all the nutrients available.

4. Bible scribes added chapters, numbers, and verses to ancient manuscripts for ease of reading and referencing. When you see a reference such as John 3:16, the first number (3) refers to the third chapter of the book of John, and the second number (16) is the verse in that chapter. The table of contents in your Bible will help you locate each book as you grow in familiarity with the Bible.

5. Each lesson contains a **Fast Forward** section where we jump ahead to the letters Peter wrote to the early Church. (Notice this is Church, with a capitol C, as opposed to

church; Church is a collective word for all Christians.) Reading Peter's words at the end of his life alongside the stories of his younger years with Jesus helps us see how much Peter changes.

6. Each lesson ends with a **One Step** section that invites you to participate in one practice of faith each week.

GUIDELINES FOR GROUPS

1. Before each session, select a person to welcome the group and read the text. Depending on the size of your group, this person, called the **Reader**, should be comfortable reading slowly, clearly, and with enough volume for the group to hear.

2. Each group session begins with a selection of Scripture from the **Weekend Reading and Reflection** study. During the reading, a word or phrase from the text will often emerge as particularly engaging for you personally. Take note of this word or phrase in the blank provided. This form of listening stems from a practice called *Lectio Divina*, which means divine readings. If yours is a large group ministry, gather first in the bigger group for the Scripture reading and teaching or testimony from someone in your group. Then break up into smaller circles.

3. After the reading, ask a teacher to reflect on the lesson or invite someone to share a personal story that relates to the Bible passage for that week. This teaching or testimony component should take about ten minutes. Alternatively, you can skip the teaching or testimony and begin the discussion questions.

4. *Lifted by Love* is written for people with different levels of familiarity with the Bible. If this is your first Bible study, resisit the urge to stay quiet to avoid sounding unknowledgeable. Often those with the least exposure to the Bible bring fresh perspectives and new insights that those with more experience often miss. Keep in mind that the goal of the discussion is not to have the right answer or to tell someone what to think, but to explore these topics together.

5. The group leader's primary job is to host the gathering and to decide how many discussion questions to cover. Depending on the talkativeness of your group, you may want to preselect the questions that fit your group best. Your job is not to facilitate the whole discussion. Each week, group members are invited to take turns reading a question, which allows everyone the option to participate in leading if they want to.

6. See www.patriciaclarke.org for more *Lifted by Love* resources.

7. Whatever is said in the group should remain confidential. No one should repeat what is shared with others outside the group.

8. Beware of the participation hangover. When you speak in a group, it is common to regret it afterward. Don't worry. This is completely normal. Brush it off and keep participating. That is how we grow.

9. If you haven't done the **Weekend Reading and Reflection** questions, you are still welcome to participate in the **Group Discussion**. The **Weekend Reading and Reflection** is helpful, but not essential for learning in the Group Discussion.

10. It is best not to speak about churches, public figures, or other religions in a negative way.

11. Be mindful of talking too much and avoid giving advice. Find a friend who will give you honest feedback if you tend to dominate conversations.

12. If you do not have a group, reflecting on and writing your answers independently will still be helpful. Finding a friend or two to join you will make it even more fun!

ICON GUIDE

 Insights and relevant content from other parts of the Bible

 The main Bible text for the week. You can look up the verses to gain familiarity with your own Bible or refer to the text printed in the lesson.

 Historical and biblical context that adds to our understanding of the text

 Scientific observations

 Observations from scholars

 Hebrew word and definition

 Greek word and definition

Lifted by Love • Lessons from the Life of Peter

WHO IS IN CHARGE?

WEEK ONE

The first serious argument my in-laws had when they were newly married was over the dishes. After dinner, Nan, my mother-in-law, left to go to a meeting and asked her husband, Boyd, to clean up. He washed the dishes, but he left the dirty pots. When Nan came home and saw the pots still on the stove, she gritted her teeth and asked, "Did you forget to do the dishes?" Confused, Boyd said, "I did. You didn't ask me to do the pots."

In an otherwise long and happy marriage, this was the first of many fights along this theme. Nan ran a tight ship as a stay-at-home mum (as they call mothers in their native Canada). With Boyd gone for work frequently and with little money to hire a babysitter, she managed three young children on a shoestring budget. She kept the house exceptionally clean, baked bread, cooked healthy meals, and raised her children in a loving way—all without complaints, self-pity, or bursts of anger when Boyd returned from a long trip. Still, as the years of motherhood and marriage passed, a growing bitterness emerged in her. *Why can't my husband and my children cooperate and do what they are told to do around the house? Why do I have to remind them to hang up their jackets and put their books away rather than dump them on the floor? Why don't the people in my life behave the way I want them to? After all, what I want for us is good!*

Although our current gender and household roles may differ from those fifty years ago, a more universal issue surfaces in this story, one we all contend with no matter if we work inside or outside the home. The subconscious position we assume when asking these universal questions is that of kingship. *I am the king, and I expect others to submit to my rule.* The point isn't for Nan to let Boyd off the hook or for him to be "king of the castle." The point is for Nan to trust God to be God. As Psalm 127:1 (ESV) says, "Unless the LORD builds the house, those who build it labor in vain." Nan's attempts to be the lord of her household proved to be frustrating, and ultimately undermined the kind of home she wanted to have by allowing resentment to eat away at her relationship with her husband.

The questions Nan asked in her heart echo the first story in the Bible about Adam and Eve in the Garden of Eden. Among the many creation narratives of the ancient world, the Genesis story is one of the few that has survived. People continue to find meaning in it today because of what it says about human nature. Adam and Eve eat the fruit that is forbidden because they want to be like God (Genesis 3:4–5). Before that, they trusted that what God said was good; after, they determined what was good and evil in their own eyes. In doing so, their souls carried a new distortion—the desire to be their own gods. That core trait replicates, like DNA, and is a part of every human's nature. We attempt to be the gods of our domains; to bend events, people, and circumstances toward our own pleasure and values; and to put ourselves at the center. When we live out this desire to be God, it creates a conflict in us and in the world around us.

Songwriter Sara Bareilles captures the idea well in her song "King of Anything." She sings, "Who cares if you disagree? You are not me." She goes on to sing, "So you dare to tell me who to be? Who died and made you king of anything?" Like my in-laws, many couples contend in a battle to rule the kingdom. On a larger scale, institutions, governments, and social systems also demonstrate this human desire to be sovereign.

In the story we're studying this week, Jesus announces that God's Kingdom is near. What does that mean? What is His Kingdom like, and what distinguishes it from human kingdoms? As we will see in the next eight weeks, God's demonstration of sovereignty is different from what Peter expects. The Kingdom Jesus establishes first disappoints Peter and then far exceeds what Peter could hope for or imagine. Ultimately, Jesus asks Peter to lay down the "kingdom of me" and invites him to live under His kingship. In God's Kingdom, the currency is love, the culture is love, and the power is love. Because love isn't demanding, Jesus doesn't overpower Peter, nor does He require submission or obedience like most human leaders. When Jesus calls Peter to be part of this Kingdom, He *invites* him into a relationship with Him. This is a new method of ruling. The nature of love is invitational and relational, not obligatory or coercive.

WEEKEND READING AND REFLECTION ONE

The Gospels refer to the first four books of the New Testament: Matthew, Mark, Luke, and John. Their authors recount the story of the life of Jesus, each told from a different perspective and to a different audience. The word *gospel* also means "good news."

Mark begins his account with a reference to Isaiah 40:3. Isaiah was a Hebrew prophet who lived about 700 years before Jesus and whose words are recorded in the Old Testament. When I visited Israel in 2018, I saw fragments of the Isaiah scroll that date back to 100 BCE. The Scriptures in the Jewish and Christian traditions have been valued, transcribed, and passed down throughout recorded history.

Read Mark 1:1–18

1. Where does John the baptizer appear? _____
   What kind of baptism does he proclaim? _____

The Greek word for *repentance* is *metanoia*. The root words are *meta*, which means "after or with," and *noeo*, which means "to perceive, to think, or the result of perceiving or thinking."

The Hebrew word for *repentance* is *teshuva*, which means "to return" or "to turn back." The Hebrew word for *sin* is *chet*, which derives from the Hebrew verb meaning "to miss the target."

2. How do the Greek and Hebrew root words for *repent*ance influence what you traditionally think about the word *repentance*?

3. Why do you think Mark begins the Gospel by linking it to the past prophecy from Isaiah? (Mark 1:1–8) What point is he making about who Jesus is?

Fun Fact: Did you know that before Israel was a country in the Middle East, it was the name of a man? The Old Testament tells the story of Jacob, who is also called Israel. He has twelve sons, and each was given land. Israel and his offspring lived in a region called Yehudah, named after one of the sons, Judah. This name evolved into the word *Jewish,* refering to the people from that family. In the Bible, God chooses the Israelites for His special purpose: so He may bless all people through them. To be God's "chosen people" conflicts with our sense of fairness, but we find this pattern repeated throughout the Bible. God calls a few in order to pour out His blessings on many. They are not chosen in order to hoard God's blessings but to bestow His blessings on the whole world.

Historical Context for Baptisms: Ancient Near East cultures commonly practiced baptisms, a ritual of water immersion for purification of sins. For the people of Israel, two historical water crossings hold significance as collective baptisms. The first occurs when the people of Israel flee their enslavement in Egypt. Led by Moses, the Israelites cross the Red Sea, which God parts and closes after them, signifying that they will never return to slavery. Then, after forty years of wandering in the wilderness, the Israelites once again cross water, this time the Jordan River. They enter the fertile land God gives them called the Promised Land. Over a thousand years later at this same River of Jordan, John performs the baptisms in this story.

4. In Mark 1:7, what does John say is different about the one who will baptize after him? _____ What part of the body does water touch? _____ What does the Holy Spirit touch? _____

5. In Mark 1:11, what are the three things Mark hears the voice from heaven say about Jesus?

_____   _____   _____

6. What story from their own history would Jewish people connect with Jesus's experience in the wilderness? (See Joshua 3:15–17.) Where do the Israelites go after their time in the wilderness? (See above about the historical context for baptisms.) Why might this parallel be significant?

The Promised Land is a real geographic territory, but it is also a metaphor that points to God's Kingdom. The *Kingdom of God* is a phrase Jesus often uses to describe "the spiritual realm over which God reigns as king, or the fulfillment on Earth of God's will."[1]

7. What is the announcement Jesus proclaims in Mark 1:15?

The Sea of Galilee is a sixty-four-square-mile lake nestled between the Golan Heights and the Galilee region in Israel. As commercial fishermen, Peter and his brother Andrew are not elite or highly educated. The text gives few details about why they leave their fishing posts, but the writer Mark indicates that Peter and the other disciples respond "at once" to Jesus's call to follow Him.

When Jesus claims that the Kingdom of God is near, He announces that the time the Israelites have been waiting for is now. What they expect, however, does not happen. They want the Messiah to lead a revolution, overthrow the oppressive Roman government, and establish God's Kingdom on earth. That the Messiah would be divine and not a human military leader would not have crossed Peter's mind. A man who is also God was as far-fetched in the first century as it is today.

8. The Jewish people have been waiting for the Messiah for a long time. Can you relate to waiting for God to show up and help? If so, in what way?

9. In Mark 1:15, Jesus issues two commands that stand as invitations, not just for the first listeners but for all people. Write those two commands here: _____ and _____. According to verse 15, why does Jesus invite those listening to these actions at this moment?

10. Before meeting Jesus, Peter is called Simon. What are Simon and his brother Andrew doing? (Mark 1:16) _____
   What command does Jesus give them? (Mark 1:17) _____
   What does Jesus say will happen? (Mark 1:17) _____

Peter fishes again, but after this story, his primary profession changes. We don't know why, but something about Jesus walking on the beach, His voice calling Peter's name, His demeanor, His commanding yet calm presence—something that can't be explained— draws Peter to Jesus. Peter leaves his nets—the ropes he touches every day, the knots he untangles each morning, the woven lines he tosses into the waves over and over again— and all that he knows, behind. When we believe in Jesus as Lord, our normal, daily patterns shift, like Peter's did. We change in fundamental ways. We may not switch professions, but when we encounter the spirit of Jesus, the spirit of His love and grace, we leave our nets and our old ways behind.

✝ Read Luke 5:1–11

11. What miracle does Jesus perform?

   What does Peter say in Luke 5:8? Why would Jesus's miracle cause Peter to say this?

Often in the summer, I sit on the beach watching fishermen cast a net over a wave as it recedes into the ocean. The technique is harder than it looks. To throw it, they grasp the middle of the net in one hand and the rest of the net with the other. It lands forming a perfect circle on the water, and then, with a simple tug, the circle collapses on itself, trapping the fish inside. It's more than a simple arm movement; it requires throwing your full body weight into the cast.

Metaphorically speaking, we do the same thing. We cast our cares into the world hoping to bring in a catch. Why do we cast our nets, and what do we try to catch? To earn income, Peter needs to throw his nets to catch fish. My mother-in-law, Nan, she threw a net of control and expectations over her family. Some of us throw our nets to catch a successful career, to find a sense of self-worth, or enough money to feel secure. Maybe we cast our nets for beauty and the approval of others, but like Peter, we throw our full body weight into this effort, only to learn that our nets aren't reliable to give us what we need.

When Peter sees the power of God manifest in Jesus—His power over the fish in the sea, the wind, and the waves—Peter falls to his knees. In the presence of such power, his eyes open to the limits of his humanity against the forces of nature. He is not in charge. God is. Similarly, in our own endeavors, we throw out nets of control, ambition, expectation, and longing over the people and circumstances in our lives. These nets often come back empty or, at best, with a meager catch, never giving us enough of what we need. To follow Jesus is to leave our old nets and live differently. How can we do that?

Fast Forward: Each week we will skip ahead and read something Peter wrote later in his life. He writes these words in a letter to the early Church: "Cast all your cares on Him, because He cares for you" (1 Peter 5:7 LSV). Casting a net is a physical representation of what it is like to cast our cares. It is a full-bodied thrust of our hearts given over to Jesus. We don't hang on to the old net of control, ambition, greed, expectations, and longings; we release it and let it go. We trust that God is God, and we are not. We trust that God is omnipotent, or all-powerful. God is in control, but take note, He is not controlling. As God's Son, Jesus initiates His Kingdom through an *invitation* to follow Him, not a show of force. Love is a radically different form of power. It is not demanding or overpowering, like we are when we are in charge. When we set aside our nets of control and cast our cares on God, we take that one step of faith to rest in God's goodness and omnipotence. In the lessons to come, let's watch what inspires Peter to repeatedly cast his cares on Jesus.

12. What are some of your cares and burdens? Cares have an emotional weight and create energy in our bodies. What do you normally do with the weight of your cares? Where does that energy go?

One Step: What are some unhealthy ways you metaphorically cast your nets or handle your cares?

As your cares surface this week, instead of lifting your old nets, what can you do to cast your cares on Jesus?

Reader: Hello, and welcome! I hope you all had a good week. For today's reading, I invite you to settle into a moment of quiet as I read Mark 1:1–18 from the New Revised Standard Version of the Bible. Listen with your imagination, and try to visualize each scene. Notice if a word, phrase, or image stands out to you.

The beginning of the good news of Jesus Christ, the Son of God.
² As it is written in the prophet Isaiah,
  "See, I am sending my messenger ahead of you,
    who will prepare your way;
  ³ the voice of one crying out in the wilderness:
    'Prepare the way of the Lord,
    make his paths straight,'"

⁴ John the baptizer appeared in the wilderness, proclaiming a baptism of repentance for the forgiveness of sins. ⁵ And people from the whole Judean countryside and all the people of Jerusalem were going out to him, and were baptized by him in the river Jordan, confessing their sins. ⁶ Now John was clothed with camel's hair, with a leather belt around his waist, and he ate locusts and wild honey. ⁷ He proclaimed, "The one who is more powerful than I is coming after me; I am not worthy to stoop down and untie the thong of his sandals. ⁸ I have baptized you with water; but he will baptize you with the Holy Spirit."

The Baptism of Jesus
⁹ In those days Jesus came from Nazareth of Galilee and was baptized by John in the Jordan. ¹⁰ And just as he was coming up out of the water, he

saw the heavens torn apart and the Spirit descending like a dove on him. [11] And a voice came from heaven, "You are my Son, the Beloved; with you I am well pleased."

The Temptation of Jesus

[12] And the Spirit immediately drove him out into the wilderness. [13] He was in the wilderness forty days, tempted by Satan; and he was with the wild beasts; and the angels waited on him.

The Beginning of the Galilean Ministry

[14] Now after John was arrested, Jesus came to Galilee, proclaiming the good news of God, [15] and saying, "The time is fulfilled, and the kingdom of God has come near; repent, and believe in the good news."

Jesus Calls the First Disciples

[16] As Jesus passed along the Sea of Galilee, he saw Simon[1*] and his brother Andrew casting a net into the sea—for they were fishermen. [17] And Jesus said to them, "Follow me and I will make you fish for people." [18] And immediately they left their nets and followed him.

Write the image, word, or phrase stands out to you.

---

[1] *Before Jesus changes his name, Peter was called Simon.

Teaching or Testimony

In this part of the meeting, invite someone from your group to speak for ten minutes, either by telling a personal story that pertains to the lesson or by teaching on the Bible passage for the week. Alternatively, you can skip this portion and go straight to the small group discussion.

Notes:

SMALL GROUP
DISCUSSION ONE

1. Hello, and welcome! In our group time, we each take a turn reading a discussion question. If you don't want to read, simply say, "I'll pass." Let's go around, introduce ourselves, and in a few words respond to this question: "What do you hope to get out of this study of Peter and this time together?"

2. Does anyone want to share the word, phrase, or image they wrote down during the reading?

3. Review two or three questions in the **Weekend Reading and Reflection** from this week that group members found interesting or important.

4. The three verbs Jesus gives His followers in this text are repent, believe, and follow. In what area of life do you feel challenged to repent of the kingdom of me and believe in the kingdom of God? What would you stop believing? What would you start believing? Write those beliefs here:

5. Later in the New Testament of the Bible, John describes the invitational nature of God's love this way: "Behold, I stand at the door and knock. If anyone hears my voice and opens the door, I will come in to him and eat with him, and he with me" (Revelation 3:20 ESV). What does this description say about God's nature and heart toward humanity?

6. In 1 Peter 5:7 (LSV), Peter writes, "Cast all your cares on him because he cares for you." This week, we practiced taking **One Step** from the unhealthy ways we handle our cares and worries. How did that go? Did anyone experience the grace of God lifting them as they took this step of faith?

Lifted by Love • Lessons from the Life of Peter

WHAT DO
I WANT?

WEEK TWO

There is no place like it. Flowers billow out of window boxes that grace the front of every house. People leave their doors unlocked day and night. With a village-like culture, locals greet each other on the cobblestone streets and chat while waiting in line at the farmstand. Places like Nantucket tempt people to believe that heaven is available here on earth, that if they only reach a little farther, they can get there. That is where my grandparents lived in the summers while I was growing up and where my family visited each August. Everything everywhere looked perfect, and my family fit in—at least, for the most part we did. My mother was eccentric. I'd grown accustomed to her oddities, but I noticed them more in the summers around the well-heeled, well-dressed islanders of Nantucket. I didn't know at the time, but her unusual nature was the beginning of what would one day be a mental health illness.

My mother resisted any form of order, which included following a recipe. Although her culinary inventions were healthy, she added unusual ingredients that made the food unappealing. There was no point in complaining about something that wouldn't change, so on vacation my siblings and I cooked together. We made delicious meals with summer tomatoes and corn from Bartlett Farm, Portuguese bread from the bakery, and fish from Island Seafood. We made the best of it, but I found myself imagining how perfect our family vacations would be *if only* my mother were more like other mothers. Sometimes I felt ashamed for wishing my mom were different, but I wished it all the same.

Years later, my siblings and I went back to Nantucket with our spouses, but without my mom. No one dressed oddly. No one cooked weird food. No one disrupted the family balance, and we all got along well. While fun and wonderful in its own way, I noticed that the if-onlys I imagined in my mind didn't go away. The absence of difficulties because she wasn't there soon filled with other if-onlys. New problems and interpersonal squabbles emerged. It was then, against the backdrop of that beautiful and nearly perfect island, that I realized that my idealized family and perfect vacation didn't exist, even when my if-only came true.

Now I experience the same faulty if-only beliefs and see their hidden presence in everyone I know. If only my spouse worked less. If only I got a promotion and made more money. If only I had new kitchen cabinets. If only this difficult person in my life changed or simply went away. We fixate on some disappointing part of life and believe that if it were different, we would arrive at a place of happiness and contentment. If only this or that changed, all would be well.

One of the stories we read this week takes place in Caesarea Philippi, a city full of shrines where travelers and locals pray to pagan gods. While most of us don't practice pagan worship as they did in the ancient world, modern gods are the objects of our if-only beliefs. They exert a potent pull on our thinking. Like pagan worshipers, our if-only thoughts reveal the belief that created things, not the Creator, have the power to give us an abundant and blessed life.

Flipping through a clothing catalog one day, I noticed this marketing slogan: "the good life." With images of happy, beautiful people lounging on a sailboat or playing beach volleyball, this brand uses our heart's desires to promote the clothing line. And guess what? It works. Even though I recognize the marketing manipulation, I'm all in! Show me a surfer or a paddler in an exotic location, and my own life looks shabby. Who doesn't want to sip a drink on the beach with friends while looking young and attractive? We want good things, and our culture teaches us what to buy and how to act to get those things. When those good things become ultimate things[2] on which we hang our highest hopes, they are no different than the shrines visited to offer sacrifices, only in this case we give away our time, energy, and money. The Bible refers to these good things we worship as *idols,* or substitute gods. We believe these created things give us the life we long for instead of worshipping the Creator of life and the giver of all good things.

What are modern-day idols we turn to as sources of life and love? While the catalog highlights the good life that most of us want, our if-only thoughts point to the deeper idols in our lives. In Nantucket, I wanted peace, security, and happiness, and at some level, I believed my idealized family would give them to me. A perfect home environment couldn't bring me a sense of wholeness then, and it can't now. Families don't have the capacity to complete us. Whether we are single, divorced, young, or old, and whether we have seemingly perfect families or clearly difficult ones, do we still worship at the shrine of a good family, wonderful kids, or the perfect marriage? And how is this any different than pagan idol worship?

If-only thinking reveals a deception that Jesus exposes for His disciples and for us today. We believe that the problem is out there, out in the circumstances of life. If only I had this _____, or if only that _____ were different, all would be well. In the early 1900s, *The Times* of London asked several influential writers to write an essay about what was wrong with the world. Well-known author G. K. Chesterton famously responded with this one short sentence: "I am."[3] Chesterton saw what Jesus saw. The problem isn't without; it is within.

In our study this week, Peter, in a city full of pagan shrines and idol worship, makes a declaration that Jesus is the Son of God. In doing so, he names Jesus as the ultimate source of life and love. When Peter proclaims that Jesus is the Messiah, he asserts that Jesus, not the "good things" of the pagans, are worthy of our worship. Good things bring pleasure, but they can't save us from ourselves. They can't bring healing and life in a world dying from the weight of our loneliness and discord. In following Jesus, Peter orients his life not around striving for good things or finding contentment in circumstances but around being a disciple of Jesus. *Disciple* means "a follower or student

> *Disciple* means "a follower or student of a teacher, leader, or philosopher."

of a teacher, leader, or philosopher." For us, what if the purpose of life is to be a disciple of God's love, to learn from it, follow it, and let it change you? What if our ultimate hope is not in living the good life but in *living a loving life?*

WEEKEND READING AND REFLECTION TWO

This week we take a whirlwind tour through four stories about Peter's life with Jesus:

1. Jesus heals Peter's mother-in-law.
2. Peter declares that Jesus is the Messiah.
3. Peter is a stumbling block.
4. Jesus is transfigured before Peter.

As we read, we will consider (1) what each event reveals about Jesus, and (2) what each event reveals about Peter.

Read Matthew 4:23–25, 8:14–15: Jesus heals Peter's mother-in-law

1. What region is Jesus traveling in? _____
   What two things does He do? _____ and _____
   What happens as a result of what he was doing?

2. What does Jesus do in Peter's house? _____
   What is the difference between a personal experience and an experience we hear or read about?

Read Matthew 16:13–28: Peter declares Jesus is the Messiah

3. What does Jesus ask the disciples in verse 13? _____
   What does he ask them in verse 15? _____

4. How does Simon Peter answer Jesus's question in verse 16? _____
   How is this similar to, but different from, what other people say?

5. John the Baptist, Elijah, Jeremiah, and other prophets were godly men, but they did not claim to be the Messiah or the Son of God. C. S. Lewis writes in his book *Mere Christianity*,

   > I am trying here to prevent anyone saying the really foolish thing that people often say about Him: "I'm ready to accept Jesus as a great moral teacher, but I don't accept His claim to be God." That is the one thing we must not say. A man who was merely a man and said the sort of things Jesus said would not be a great moral teacher. He would either be a lunatic—on a level with the man who says he is a poached egg—or else he would be the Devil of Hell. You must make your choice. Either this man was, and is, the Son of God: or else a madman or something worse. You can shut Him up for a fool, you can spit at Him and kill Him as a demon; or you can fall at His feet and call him Lord and God. But let us not come with any patronising nonsense about His being a great human teacher. He has not left that open to us. He did not intend to.[4]

   How is your life impacted differently if you believe Jesus was a good moral teacher but not the Lord?

6. *Disciple* means "a follower or pupil of a teacher, leader, or philosopher."[5] What is the difference between believing in Jesus and being a disciple of Jesus?

"Son of Man" is a term from a dream Daniel in the Old Testament had. Daniel 7:13–14 says, "In my vision at night I looked, and there before me was one like a son of man, coming with the clouds of heaven. He approached the Ancient of Days and was led into his presence. He was given authority, glory and sovereign power; all nations and peoples of every language worshiped him. His dominion is an everlasting dominion that will not pass away, and his kingdom is one that will never be destroyed." At times, the Bible refers to Jesus as the Son of Man, emphasizing His humanity and His fulfillment of Daniel's vision. At other times, Jesus allows Himself to be called the Son of God, emphasizing His divinity.

7. Why are Jesus's divinity and humanity so important?

8. According to Jesus, how did Simon come to this understanding? (Matthew 16:17) _____ What new name does Jesus give him, and what promise does He make? (Matthew 16:18) _____ Does "this rock" refer to Peter or to Peter's confession?

The Greek word for *rock* is *petra*, which is also translated "shelf of rock or rocks."[6]

The city of Caesarea Philippi has a river that flows from an underground spring. It is believed to be an opening to Hades, or the place of the dead. So Jesus's statement that the "gates of Hades would not prevail" has particular relevance at this location.

9. In Matthew 16:21–26, it becomes clear that Jesus and Peter have different understandings about the role of the Messiah. What does Peter object to about what Jesus is saying?

10. Peter trusts Jesus as the Messiah, but he also has expectations of what Jesus will do for him. Timothy Keller writes in his book *King's Cross*:

> Jesus will not be a means to an end; he will not be used. If he calls you to follow him, he must be the goal. Does that sound like fanaticism? Not if you understand the difference between religion and the gospel. Remember

what religion is: advice on how you must live to earn your way to God…The gospel isn't advice: It's the good news that you don't need to earn your way to God; Jesus has already done it for you. And it's a gift that you receive by sheer grace—through God's thoroughly unmerited favor.[7]

What Jesus brings is the opposite of religion. Still, even those who believe in the gospel of grace often revert to a religious mindset. We attempt to *earn* our way into God's good grace and think then our life will be blessed. How do we see Peter's religious mindset?

Why do you think we are prone to live with a religious mindset rather than one of giving and receiving unmerited love?

11. In Matthew 16:18–19, Jesus names Peter as a rock for the church, but in Matthew 16:23, he refers to him as a different kind of rock. What kind of rock is he now?

What mistake of mindset does Jesus tell Peter he has made in Matthew 16:23?

_____

What human hopes might Peter have for the Messiah?

12. Starting in Matthew 16:24, Jesus describes what it means to follow Him. What are the three things we must do?

_____, _____, and _____

Even though Peter trusts Jesus, he does what so many of us Christians do: we barter with God. We give Him our good behavior in exchange for a blessed life. We use God as a means to an end rather than worship God because He is worthy of worship—He is the only one whose very nature is life and love.

13. Write Matthew 16:25 here.

Consider how someone might lose his or her life while trying to gain it. When we worship what isn't worth our worship, we become its slave. An idol steals the very thing it promises to give. Look at the following examples:

1. If we orient our lives around money, we never think we have enough.
2. If we orient our lives around beauty, we never feel pretty.
3. If we orient our lives around success, we never feel good enough.
4. If we orient our lives around security, we never feel safe.
5. If we orient our lives around ideal relationships, we suffocate the ones we love.
6. If we orient our lives around having ideal children, we harm them by over-parenting and we burden them with our expectations.

Can you think of your own examples?

Read Mark 9:2–8

14. This is an account of Jesus being transfigured before Peter. Who is in this inner circle of disciples, and what does Jesus show them?

What does Peter say in Mark 9:5?

Why do you think Peter wants to contain and sustain the presence of the divine? In what ways does religion do that?

Fast Forward to 1 Peter 2:4–5 (NRSV). Peter writes this invitation to the early Church: "Come to him, a living stone, though rejected by mortals yet chosen and precious in God's sight, and like living stones, let yourselves be built into a spiritual house." In what way does Peter use the imagery of a house and stones? What might be the purpose of this house, and how are we invited to be part of it? (There is not one right answer to this question. Use your imagination!)

One Step: What is a way you could worship God this week? Circle a suggestion listed below, or write your own.

1. Each morning, reflect on the previous day and write a gratitude list of three things that happened.
2. Take a walk in nature.
3. Do something creative that brings you joy.
4. Listen to, sing, or play worship music.
5. Perform a random act of kindness for a stranger.
6. Enjoy a meal or beverage with close friends.

7.

8.

Reader: Hello, and welcome! I hope you all had a good week. For today's reading, I invite you to settle into a moment of quiet while I read Matthew 16:13–28. Listen with your imagination, and try to visualize the scene. See if a word, phrase, or image stands out to you.

Matthew 16:13–28 (NRSV)

[13] Now when Jesus came into the district of Caesarea Philippi, he asked his disciples, "Who do people say that the Son of Man is?" [14] And they said, "Some say John the Baptist, but others Elijah, and still others Jeremiah or one of the prophets." [15] He said to them, "But who do you say that I am?" [16] Simon Peter answered, "You are the Messiah, the Son of the living God." [17] And Jesus answered him, "Blessed are you, Simon son of Jonah! For flesh and blood has not revealed this to you, but my Father in heaven. [18] And I tell you, you are Peter, and on this rock I will build my church, and the gates of Hades will not prevail against it. [19] I will give you the keys of the kingdom of heaven, and whatever you bind on earth will be bound in heaven, and whatever you loose on earth will be loosed in heaven." [20] Then he sternly ordered the disciples not to tell anyone that he was the Messiah.

Jesus Foretells His Death and Resurrection

[21] From that time on, Jesus began to show his disciples that he must go to Jerusalem and undergo great suffering at the hands of the elders and chief priests and scribes, and be killed, and on the third day be raised. [22] And Peter took him aside and began to rebuke him, saying, "God forbid it, Lord! This must never happen to you." [23] But he turned and said to Peter, "Get

behind me, Satan! You are a stumbling block to me; for you are setting your mind not on divine things but on human things."

The Cross and Self-Denial

[24] Then Jesus told his disciples, "If any want to become my followers, let them deny themselves and take up their cross and follow me. [25] For those who want to save their life will lose it, and those who lose their life for my sake will find it. [26] For what will it profit them if they gain the whole world but forfeit their life? Or what will they give in return for their life?

[27] "For the Son of Man is to come with his angels in the glory of his Father, and then he will repay everyone for what has been done. [28] Truly I tell you, there are some standing here who will not taste death before they see the Son of Man coming in his kingdom."

Write the image, word, or phrase that stands out to you: _____

Teaching or Testimony

(optional)

Notes:

SMALL GROUP
DISCUSSION TWO

1. Does anyone want to share their word, phrase, or image? Review two or three questions from this week's **Weekend Reading and Reflection** that group members found interesting or important.

2. What are three ways rocks are mentioned in the readings from this week? How are they used in different ways?

📖 **Read Matthew 16:24–25**

3. What do you think this verse means?

4. In the last two stories, we watch Peter do what we often do when we become religious:

- Expect certain outcomes from God because of our devotion.
- Attempt to contain the mystery and majesty of God.

Why do we do this?

How do worship and wonder serve as anecdotes for our attempts to control God?

5. Read and review the **One Step** for the week. How did that go? Do any of you want to share a story of God *lifting* you as you stepped out in faith or started to sink?

WHO DO I TRUST?

WEEK THREE

t was the summer of 2016, and I was sitting by the pool while the children dove for pennies and practiced handstands. With all of them swimming, I enjoyed what new mothers dream of—reading a book or a magazine while on vacation. The air felt unusually cool for July as I settled onto a lounge chair with my Kindle and iced tea. Hardly any time went by before I noticed some storm clouds rolling in. Soon, a few raindrops landed on my shoulders, and I moved under the pergola. The kids wanted to stay in the pool, so I grabbed a few towels and wrapped myself up, thinking it was merely an afternoon sprinkle. Then the rain started coming faster. The towels became damp, keeping me wet rather than dry. In the pool that had earlier been heated by the sun, the children stayed warm and didn't mind at all. Meanwhile, I was shivering.

It dawned on me that the rain was a metaphor for something I do often—I attempt to avoid the unavoidable. Whether it's the problem I ignore, the grief I can't face, the disappointments I won't name, or the conflict I avoid, what I resist persists.

When we are growing up, we acquire our own set of personal coping skills to navigate the rough waters of responsibility and the hard knocks of life. If we are averse to conflict, for example, we might make peace to force the conflict to go away. Like the futility of towels in a rainstorm, however, we internalize our thoughts. A simmering bitterness grows, and the conflict remains. Or maybe we blow up, yell, and intimidate our opponent, but the conflict remains. The same holds true for perfectionism and people-pleasing. Both deny an uncomfortable reality that exists whether we like it or not. Perfection doesn't change the inevitable messiness of life, and while people-pleasing prevents conflict, it inhibits authenticity, a key ingredient for intimacy and friendship.

Our skills may differ, but we, like Peter, construct a boat to float above the deep waters of uncertainty in order to survive. The boat feels safe because it is familiar, and we are in control. Rowing the boat is necessary and good, until one day it isn't. The boat's job is to keep us dry and afloat, but with some storms it isn't up to the task. We come to a point where our tools for life, the ones we honed for years, no longer serve us well. The depth of the hull is no match for the height of the waves. We have the chance to step into a new way of living, one built on faith and love, not our acquired tools for power, control, and security. For Peter on the lake and for me by the pool, the storm can't be controlled, subdued, or overpowered. It is a reality. Rather than crouch in the bottom of the boat or wrap in towels under a pergola, we must step *into* the storm.

For Peter to follow Jesus, to abandon his old way of life, he needs to know who Jesus is—not just in his mind, in his theology, or in his religious practices but in his physical body. He needs to feel the smack of the waves hitting his shins, to know the wind's gale against his chest, to taste the fear of sinking into the dark waters below, and to risk it all on Jesus's claim to be the Lord of heaven and earth. For Peter, he needs to leave the boat to know that Jesus is God. The question is this: *Do we need to do the same?*

In these lines from her poem "Unconditional," Jennifer Paine Welwood captures the transformation that happens when we step out of the boat, face what we avoid, entrust ourselves to God, and allow His divine love to lift us.

> Willing to experience aloneness,
> I discover connection everywhere . . .
> Opening to my loss,
> I gain the embrace of the universe;
> Surrendering into emptiness,
> I find fullness without end.
> Each condition I flee from pursues me,
> Each condition I welcome transforms me.

WEEKEND READING AND REFLECTION THREE

What is Peter's daily life like? As a professional fisherman, Peter's livelihood depends on both hard work and luck. Some days the weather cooperates, and other days a storm prevents him from catching anything at all. At times, Peter and his brother fish all night (John 21:3), a choice not born from ambition but necessity or even desperation. In the first century, a fisherman doesn't accumulate enough wealth for long-term security; he fishes for daily resources to live and survive. He controls his income with skill, effort, and his boat; but he can't control nature.

The political climate for Peter and his family is as unpredictable as the wind on the Sea of Galilee. For Jewish people, Roman control leads to widespread concern for their safety and the vitality of the Jewish customs. The situation is sometimes mild and sometimes violent, depending on the ruler assigned to their region. One tetrarch, Archelaus, begins his rule by slaughtering 3,000 people during the Jewish Passover.[8] Such instability casts a shadow of fear over the Jewish people as they live under Roman authority.

Read Matthew 14:22–36

1. What miracle precedes this section? _____
   What does Jesus do after being with a lot of people? _____

2. What time does Jesus appear to the disciples? (Matthew 14:25) _____
   He walks toward them from the eastern side of the lake. What would be behind Jesus, and how would He look? _____

At the time, people believed the souls of those who died at sea wandered over the waters where they died. The Sea of Galilee was not very big, but it was a body of water surrounded by hills. Storms hit suddenly and could devastate a small vessel. A typical fishing boat measured twenty-seven feet long, about as long as a London bus.

3. How do the disciples feel when they see Jesus? (Matthew 14:26)

    What does Jesus say? (Matthew 14:27) "Take heart, _____

The Greek translation for "it is I" is the same as the word used for "I am" in Exodus 3:14. God speaks those words to Moses, the man who leads the Israelites out of slavery: "But Moses said to God, 'Who am I that I should go to Pharaoh, and bring the sons of Israel out of Egypt?' He said, 'I will be with you; and this shall be the sign for you that it is I who sent you: when you have brought the people out of Egypt, you shall worship God on this mountain.' But Moses said to God, 'If I come to the Israelites and say to them, "The God of your ancestors has sent me to you," and they ask me, "What is his name?" what shall I say to them?' God said to Moses, 'I AM WHO I AM.' He said further, 'Thus you shall say to the Israelites, "The LORD, the God of Jacob, has sent me to you"'" (Exodus 3:11–14).

4. What is Jesus saying about Himself when he says, "It is I, do not be afraid."?

5. What does Peter ask Jesus to do in Matthew 14:28? _____
    What does Jesus say in response in Matthew 14:29? _____

6. When you read about a miracle in the Bible, what is your level of skepticism?

    Is this miracle as shocking for the disciples as it would be for us today? _____
    If so, how do we know that from the text? _____

About miracles, New Testament scholar and historian Dr. N. T. Wright writes:

We are right then to be astonished; but not to do what so many in the last two hundred years have done, and elevate that astonishment into a critical principle, ruling out from our world (and that of Jesus) anything that breaks what we think of as laws of nature. Nor is this a plea to allow for "supernature" or "supernaturalism", as though there were simply a different force which might invade our world from outside. Rather, we are invited to see something more mysterious by far: a dimension *of* our world which is normally hidden, which had indeed died, but which Jesus brings to new life.[9]

As we consider miracles, here are some questions to ponder: Do we want to believe in a God of miracles?

If not, why not?

If so, why?

7. Let's zoom in on that moment when Peter has one foot in the boat and one foot over the side of the boat, touching the water (Matthew 14:29–31). What words describe how each foot feels?

Put Each Word in the Appropriate Column	Water	Boat
Firm		
Not solid		
Safe		
Risky		
Understandable		
Uncomprehendable		
Familiar		
Comfortable		
New experience		
Scary		
Made by Peter		
Made by God		
Controllable		
Mysterious and unknown		

8. Consider the expression "a step of faith" and the various contexts in which we hear those words. What does taking a step of faith entail? _____

_____

What immediately follows Peter's step of faith? _____

What does Peter say when he starts to sink? _____

What does Jesus say to Peter? _____

The boat provides security against the wind and the waves, and yet Peter *asks* Jesus to command him to get out of the boat. Why do you think he does that? Why does he *ask Jesus to ask him* rather than simply get out of the boat?

_____

_____

Read Matthew 17:20 (LSV)

"For truly I say to you, if you may have faith as a grain of mustard, you will say to this mountain, Move from here to there, and it will move; and nothing will be impossible to you."

According to this verse and this story about Peter, what is important about faith?

_____

What is less important? _____

9. What does Jesus do when Peter cries out to Him? _____

This gesture parallels an experience described by the author of Psalm 18.

Read Psalm 18:16–19 (NIV)

He reached down from on high and took hold of me;
   he drew me out of deep waters.
He rescued me from my powerful enemy,
   from my foes, who were too strong for me.

They confronted me in the day of my disaster,
    but the LORD was my support.
He brought me out into a spacious place;
    he rescued me because he delighted in me.

In the Psalms, the word *enemy* refers to a military foe, but as modern readers, our enemies take more obscure forms. Our enemies look like discouragement, loneliness, sickness, difficulty in a relationship, or feeling stuck at work. Other times, our adversary is busyness or obsessive thinking about a particular problem. When a close friend of mine struggled with cancer, we regularly prayed against her enemies, which were the cancer cells attempting to gain ground in her body. Whether it is a disease, an addiction, an injustice, a failing marriage, a difficult job, or a hurting child, the book of Psalms invites us to bring our full range of human emotions to God. It is a prayer collection giving us permission to lay down the worst and best of ourselves at God's feet.

10. What enemy threatens you today?

Boat Assessment Tool

Imagine yourself in this scene on the Sea of Galilee. Write words on the drawing of the boat that describe how you typically handle the storms of life, even the small daily storms. Write words on the waves that describe what overwhelms you.

Boat Assessment Tool

11. The Barnabas Counseling Center uses the letter **D** as a tool to help us understand the unhealthy ways we react to **Disappointment**. We turn to one or more of the three **D**s: **Despair**, **Deny**, or **Demand**. How do you most often respond to life's disappointments? For a-c, respond with Never, Sometimes, or Often.

    a. Do you give way to *despair*? _____

    b. Do you escape into work or fun and *deny* anything is wrong? _____

    c. Do you *demand* more from yourself and those around you? _____

    d. Is *dependance* on God (a positive **D**) the response Peter has? _____

12. What **D** strategy do you employ when the waves come? How would dependance on God change this response?

13. How is the boat you've built working? How does it affect your relationships for better or for worse? Your work? Your health?

14. **Fast Forward** to 2 Peter 1:5–7. Here we find a substructure of a loving life.

    > [5] For this very reason, make every effort to add to your faith goodness; and to goodness, knowledge; [6] and to knowledge, self-control; and to self-control, perseverance; and to perseverance, godliness; [7] and to godliness, mutual affection; and to mutual affection, love.

    What is the first item listed? _____
    Why is faith the foundation?

One Step: Peter says, "Lord, if it is you, command me to come to you on the water." Jesus says, "Come" (Matthew 14:28–29 NRSV). In what way is Jesus inviting you to step out of your boat in faith?

Peter needed to *trust in order to trust.* As you step out toward Jesus, what might this phrase mean to you?

What doubts and fears accompany this step for you?

Reader: For today's reading, I invite you to settle in for a moment of quiet and hear the text for today: Matthew 14:22–36. Listen to see if a word or phrase resonates with you.

Read Matthew 14:22–36 (NRSV)

22 Immediately he made the disciples get into the boat and go on ahead to the other side, while he dismissed the crowds. 23 And after he had dismissed the crowds, he went up the mountain by himself to pray. When evening came, he was there alone, 24 but by this time the boat, battered by the waves, was far from the land, for the wind was against them. 25 And early in the morning he came walking toward them on the sea. 26 But when the disciples saw him walking on the sea, they were terrified, saying, "It is a ghost!" And they cried out in fear. 27 But immediately Jesus spoke to them and said, "Take heart, it is I; do not be afraid."

28 Peter answered him, "Lord, if it is you, command me to come to you on the water." 29 He said, "Come." So Peter got out of the boat, started walking on the water, and came toward Jesus. 30 But when he noticed the strong wind, he became frightened, and beginning to sink, he cried out, "Lord, save me!" 31 Jesus immediately reached out his hand and caught him, saying to him, "You of little faith, why did you doubt?" 32 When they got into the boat, the wind ceased. 33 And those in the boat worshiped him, saying, "Truly you are the Son of God."

Write the image, word, or phrase stands out to you: _____

Teaching or Testimony
(optional)

Notes:

SMALL GROUP
DISCUSSION THREE

1. Does anyone want to share the word or phrase that stood out to you?

2. Review two to three questions in the **Weekend Reading and Reflection** that group members found interesting or important.

📖 **Read Psalm 18:16–19 (NIV)**

3. Psalm 18:16–19 (NIV) has strong parallels to this week's story with Peter.

> He reached down from on high and took hold of me;
> he drew me out of deep waters.
> He rescued me from my powerful enemy,
> from my foes, who were too strong for me.
> They confronted me in the day of my disaster,
> but the Lord was my support.
> He brought me out into a spacious place;
> he rescued me because he delighted in me.

List together the seven things God does in this psalm.

    1.

2.

3.

4.

5.

6.

7.

According to the text, why does God rescue them?

What are some "powerful enemies" we face today?

4. What does it mean that *we must trust in order to trust*? How does taking a step of faith increase our capacity to experience God's *love as trustworthy*?

5. Review the **One Step** for the week. How did it go? Do any of you want to share a story of God *lifting* you as you stepped out in faith or started to sink?

AM I GOOD ENOUGH?

WEEK FOUR

"Where are you going?" my mom asked as she walked past my doorway to put my little brother to bed.

"The usual," I said. "We are spending the night at Corey's."

"Are her parents at home?" she asked.

"Of course, Mom. I know the rules." I put in my gold earrings, the ones I wore when dressing up, and finished blow drying my hair.

For the most part, I was a good kid. I thought of myself as someone who always told the truth, but on that night I lied. In high school, I hung out with my best friends, Corey and Rachel, whenever I could. After school, they went to cheerleading practice and I went to soccer practice, but on the weekends we were inseparable. With good snacks and a nice vibe, Corey's house was our usual hangout spot for a sleepover, so my parents were used to this routine. This time, though, Corey's parents were traveling. We knew if we slept there we could stay out late at a party and our parents would never know. As I finished getting dressed, guilt nagged at me, but I thought to myself, *Everyone lies to their parents occasionally. And everyone is going to this party. It will be fine.*

In the big scheme of my life, nothing terrible happened at that party, but just as one small choice leads to another, my decision to deceive my parents initiated a series of other bad decisions. During the night, I met an older boy who I'd later start dating against my better judgement. After several months he broke up with me to get back together with his ex-girlfriend. He picked someone else over me and the rejection broke my heart. The least happy and most volatile months of my adolescence followed that party, and I trace it all back to that one night. If I hadn't ignored my gut instinct, if I hadn't blatantly lied to my parents, I would never have met that boy and I would have been spared that tumultuous time. My conscience tried to warn me, but I didn't listen.

As an adult, however, I don't regret going to the party because the lesson serves me well today. My conscience is not like a finger-wagging buzz kill, but a wise friend who is to be trusted. Ignoring her leads to trouble and heartache. That mistake still shapes me in important ways. I know to not trust the insistent voice that says *everyone is going* but to listen to the quieter one that invites me to wonder what my gut is warning me about.

Paradoxically, mistakes teach me *not* to trust myself and at the same time *how* to trust myself. They teach me to question my motives, thoughts, and desires. Proverbs 21:2 (NLT) says, "People may be right in their own eyes, but the LORD examines their heart." We need help to see our hearts more clearly. Telling the truth to others is the easy part. Telling the truth to yourself is where the real work begins. God uses our personal failures to teach us. He repurposes our mistakes as stepping stones to make us wise.

The same is true for Peter. His mistakes and failures make him *more—not less—* qualified for the work Jesus has for him. Peter's passionate nature leads to overconfidence in himself. He gets ahead of himself. His betrayal, however, thrusts him back into a place of humility. And in the Kingdom of God, humility is the essential ingredient for leadership. In the context of forgiveness and grace, Peter's worst moment transforms him into his best self.

Paul, another writer in the New Testament, says this about God in 2 Corinthians 12:9–10 (NRSV): "But he [God] said to me, 'My grace is sufficient for you, for my power is made perfect in weakness.' Therefore I will boast all the more gladly about my weaknesses, so that Christ's power may rest on me. That is why, for Christ's sake, I delight in weaknesses, in insults, in hardships, in persecutions, in difficulties. For when I am weak, then I am strong."

Peter's failure at a pivotal moment causes his confidence in his ego to die and enables his faith in Jesus to grow. In this way, Jesus demonstrates His strength through Peter's weakness. Without a humble posture, Peter can't be the rock, the *petra*, on which the church is built. Without a humble posture, Peter promotes his own mission for Jesus rather than trusting Jesus's mission for the world. Without a humble posture, Peter would seek to be loved and praised for his leadership, rather than use his leadership to bring love and praise to God in the way that Jesus models.

WEEKEND READING AND REFLECTION FOUR

Passover is a holiday when the Jewish people remember their liberation from slavery in Egypt in the thirteenth century BC. In Exodus, the second book of the Bible, God helps the children of Israel escape their enslavement by inflicting ten plagues on the Egyptians. The tenth and worst plague brought death to the firstborn Egyptian sons. In advance, Moses tells the Israelites to mark the doorframes of their homes with the blood of a slaughtered lamb. Upon seeing the marking, the spirit of death will "pass over," sparing the firstborn son in that home. That is why the holiday is called Passover. The story for this lesson takes place during the Passover feast.

Read Luke 22:7–23

1. Who does Jesus ask to prepare the Passover meal? (Luke 22:8) _____
Jesus states that He wants to eat the Passover meal with the disciples before He does what (Luke 22:15)? _____
He claims that He will not drink wine again until what happens? _____
_____

Suffering and establishing the Kingdom of God don't seem to fit together. Why would this confuse the disciples?

2. In Luke 22:19–20, what does Jesus do with His hands? _____,
_____, and _____.
What words does He say? _____
What does He say happens to His body? _____
Who is this for? _____

3. Consider the words given for you and poured out for you (Luke 22:19–20). How does the history behind Passover help us understand what Jesus is saying here?

Who is the new lamb Jesus is talking about?

4. Complete this sentence: This cup that is poured out for you is the

At the Last Supper (a term used to describe this Passover gathering before Jesus's death), Jesus announces a new covenant. To understand the significance of this statement, let's look at the old covenant. Ancient covenants serve as legal agreements between two parties, binding them together as closely as blood bonds a family. Today, we find such agreements in a wedding ceremony or when an adoption takes place. Historically, the two parties would cut an animal in half and walk between the halves, symbolizing the death that should happen if either party breaks the covenant. The old covenant refers to the agreement God makes with Moses on behalf of the Israelites. God promises to bring peace and blessing to the Isrealites, and in return the Isrealites agree to uphold the law given to Moses. To maintain the covenant, the Israelites offer yearly animal sacrifices to atone for the ways they do not uphold their end of the treaty.

5. What do you think Jesus means when He says, "This cup is the new covenant in my blood, which is poured out for you"?

6. Why does the new covenant no longer require animal sacrifices?

† **Read Luke 22:24–28**

7. Jesus speaks of His body and blood in a way that perplexes the disciples. Afterward, what do they begin arguing about? _____

   What does Jesus say that His new Kingdom looks like?

8. What does Jesus confer on the disciples that God has conferred on Jesus?

† **Read Luke 22:32–34**

9. Why does Jesus pray for Peter's faith not to fail instead of just praying that Peter doesn't fail?[10] What is the difference?

10. What does Jesus expect will happen to Peter first? Second?

† **Read Luke 22: 39–46**

11. What does Jesus pray? _____
    What words in this prayer represent His desire? _____
    What words in this prayer represent His trust in His Father? _____
    How is this short prayer both encouraging and challenging to us in how we talk to God? _____

12. What are the disciples doing when Jesus returns?

13. What two things does Jesus tell them to do? _____, _____
    What do those two things prevent? _____

Can you relate to "checking out" when you don't want to face life's demands?[11] Napping isn't for everyone, but it's a favorite pastime of mine. I can fall asleep in a chair, in a waiting room, at the beach—you name it. In the most stressful times, I often take a powernap in order to cope. If not sleep, what is your go-to activity when you are shutting down and avoiding a challenging situation?

Does it make you feel better that even the disciples can't rise to every occasion; that they, like us, don't always have the courage to face a discouraging situation? Still, eventually we must deal what is in front of us. Like the disciples, we need to wake up, be brave, and meet life on life's terms. We can't outrun reality. At those times, Jesus invites us to get up and pray, "For God did not give us a spirit of cowardice, but rather a spirit of power and of love and of self-discipline" (2 Timothy 1:7 NRSV). In these times, we take comfort knowing Jesus also faces insurmountable challenges. We can join with Him in praying, "Take this cup from me; yet not my will, but yours be done" (Luke 22:42 NIV).

Read Luke 22:47–62

14. In John's account of this same incident, Peter cuts off the high priest's right ear (John 18:10). What adjectives would you use to describe this aspect of Peter's personality?

Where else have we seen these traits in Peter?

15. Why do you think Peter is in the courtyard, and what do you believe he is thinking?

16. Association with Jesus endangers Peter's life. What does this show about Peter that he takes this risk?

17. What two things happen immediately after Peter's denials?

18. At first the crowing of the rooster seems like a haunting and condemning sound, but keep in mind that the crowing is a sound Peter will hear morning and night for the rest of his life. William Hendrikson says, "This hidden memory will pull the rope that will ring the bell of Peter's conscience."[12] How could the rooster be a daily reminder of grace for Peter going forward?

19. At dinner, Peter promises to follow Jesus to His death. Now he denies Jesus, not once, not twice, but three times. Peter doesn't believe he is capable of such betrayal, and yet here he is repeatedly denying any association with Jesus. Like so many of us, a disconnect exists between Peter's desires and his actions. He has competing passions—love for Jesus and desire for self-protection. In the end, his innate instinct for self-preservation wins out. He denies Jesus. When we say or do something we regret, self-loathing kicks in. We dislike ourselves for our mistakes. We obsess over how badly we mess up. Have you ever regretted something significant that you did or said? If so, what do you do when you feel ashamed?

How might Peter feel when he realizes what he has done?

Fast Forward to 1 Peter 1:6–7 (NRSV). Peter writes this: "For a little while you have had to suffer various trials, so that the genuineness of your faith—being more precious than gold that, though perishable, is tested by fire—may be found to result in praise and glory and honor when Jesus Christ is revealed." What do you think this verse means?

A medalsmith softens gold in a fire so that it can be reshaped for a new purpose. How does Peter's trial, which ironically takes place during Jesus's trial, soften him and reshape his faith into something stronger?

Repentance: To have the courage to admit our failures and receive God's grace is to learn to repent. Learning to repent is one of the greatest skills we can acquire and without it our past mistakes produce shame. Rather than motivating positive change, shame reinforces our negative behavior. Repentance is not a religious "ought to." It is a gift from God, a loving "get to." The practice of repentance breaks the power of shame.

The steps of repentance are:

1. *Turn* to God and tell Him about what you did that you regret.
2. *Repent* and ask God for help. Take heart. Our sin is bigger than we think, but God's love is greater than we can imagine.
3. *Receive* His grace and forgiveness.
4. *Trust* you are loved by God. Ask God to help you change.
5. *Release* any shame you feel.

One Step: Staying in the boat means wallowing in shame. *Stepping* out of the boat means repenting and receiving the grace of Jesus. This week practice repentance instead of self-criticism. Is there anything you need to repent of today? If so, write a repentance prayer using the steps here:

Repentance Prayer

Reader: Hello, and welcome! I hope you all had a good week. For today's reading, I invite you settle into a moment of quiet while I read Luke 22:14–34. Listen for a word or phrase that stands out to you.

Luke 22:14–34 (NRSV)

[14] When the hour came, he took his place at the table, and the apostles with him. [15] He said to them, "I have eagerly desired to eat this Passover with you before I suffer; [16] for I tell you, I will not eat it until it is fulfilled in the kingdom of God." [17] Then he took a cup, and after giving thanks he said, "Take this and divide it among yourselves; [18] for I tell you that from now on I will not drink of the fruit of the vine until the kingdom of God comes." [19] Then he took a loaf of bread, and when he had given thanks, he broke it and gave it to them, saying, "This is my body, which is given for you. Do this in remembrance of me." [20] And he did the same with the cup after supper, saying, "This cup that is poured out for you is the new covenant in my blood. [21] But see, the one who betrays me is with me, and his hand is on the table. [22] For the Son of Man is going as it has been determined, but woe to that one by whom he is betrayed!" [23] Then they began to ask one another which one of them it could be who would do this.

The Dispute about Greatness

[24] A dispute also arose among them as to which one of them was to be regarded as the greatest. [25] But he said to them, "The kings of the Gentiles lord it over them; and those in authority over them are called benefactors. [26] But not so with you; rather the greatest among you must become like the youngest, and the leader like one who serves. [27] For who is greater, the one

who is at the table or the one who serves? Is it not the one at the table? But I am among you as one who serves.

28 "You are those who have stood by me in my trials; 29 and I confer on you, just as my Father has conferred on me, a kingdom, 30 so that you may eat and drink at my table in my kingdom, and you will sit on thrones judging the twelve tribes of Israel.

Jesus Predicts Peter's Denial

31 "Simon, Simon, listen! Satan has demanded to sift all of you like wheat, 32 but I have prayed for you that your own faith may not fail; and you, when once you have turned back, strengthen your brothers." 33 And he said to him, "Lord, I am ready to go with you to prison and to death!" 34 Jesus said, "I tell you, Peter, the cock will not crow this day, until you have denied three times that you know me."

Write an image, word, or phrase stands out to you: _____

Teaching or Testimony

(optional)

Notes:

SMALL GROUP
DISCUSSION FOUR

1. Does anyone want to share the word, phrase, or image they wrote down during the reading?

2. Review two to three questions in the **Weekend Reading and Reflection** from this week that group members found interesting or important.

3. What does Jesus say specifically about His body at the Last Supper? (Luke 22:19)

   How do these words shed new light on the prayer, "Give us this day our daily bread"?

4. What does it mean when Jesus says that this cup "is the new covenant in my blood"? (Luke 22:20 NIV)

How does the new covenant change the ancient practice of sacrifice to the practice of repentance?

5. What is the purpose of sifting wheat? How are failures and mistakes important for Peter's leadership in the kingdom of God? (Luke 22:31–32)

Read Luke 22:54-62 and Romans 8:1 (NRSV)
"There is therefore now no condemnation for those who are in Christ Jesus."

6. How can self-condemnation lead to a cycle of failure?

7. Review the **One Step** for the week. How did this go? Do any of you want to share a story of God *lifting* you as stepped out in faith or started to sink?

WHAT IS LOVE?

According to the first law of thermodynamics, energy in a closed system is neither lost nor found; it is transferred. The same law of physics applies to emotions in humans within the closed system of humanity. The energy of hate or love isn't lost or found; it is merely transferred. An emotional and spiritual connection exists among humans, and emotions, like energy, are neither lost nor found; they are transferred. Our emotional energy doesn't disappear; it goes somewhere. Anger leads to anger. Irritation leads to irritation. Generosity leads to generosity. Sometimes it is transferred to another person, sometimes it is absorbed into our own bodies, sometimes it is burned off at the gym or reshaped into art, and sometimes it festers into disease—but it never disappears. What we find at the epicenter of Christianity, however, is a conversion of energy. Like an alchemist turns base metals into gold, Christ on the cross transforms hate into love.

On March 22, 2020, I drove to Charlottesville, Virginia, with some friends to hear John M. Perkins, a civil rights leader, give his farewell speech at the University of Virginia (UVA). Perkins's ninety years of life as a minister, activist, best-selling author, community developer, and member of Presidential task forces convey more than words he could say from the stage. Perkins delivered his speech with strength and grace. He wove Scripture seamlessly into every thought, as if the words of the Bible were sewn into his heart and mind, holding him together like stitches on a patchwork quilt. What stood out to me most was not what he said but what his life says. I wondered what enabled him to forgive the jailers who beat him and left him to die for a crime he never committed. When he recounted the story, he said, "In that moment, I thought I could never like any white folk again."

But then he did. He found the ability to love all of us in that UVA Dome Room, a space built to honor Thomas Jefferson. Where did all the energy of hate and shame go? In the beating, the jailers pounded their hate into Mr. Perkins, but then where did it go from there? How did it stop? Forgiveness is the simple answer, but it is not the full story. For Perkins, the hatred the jailers assailed him with, blow by blow, passed *through* forgiveness and then converted to love. Where did he find the strength to love under the force of such evil? That remarkable love is Christ's love. What Jesus did on the cross is more than forgiveness; it is conversion.

On Good Friday, we remember Jesus's death for the forgiveness of our sins. In her famous three-hour sermon in St. Thomas Church in New York City on March 30, 2018,

Fleming Rutledge, Episcopal priest and author, spoke about what the crucifixion of Jesus *achieves*.[13] His death is more than forgiveness; He makes the ungodly godly. This basic doctrine, the epicenter of Christianity, boggles the mind. *How?* How does the historical death of Jesus make a person godly 2,000 years later? How does this transformation work? What does it look like?

On the cross, Jesus endures relentless betrayal, mockery, and violence. If each human emotion on that darkened day were drawn like lines on a paper, Jesus's body would resemble an airport map with many arrivals and few departures. Every gesture of hate descended on his body at once. Only two times does Jesus react: once with a request, "Father, forgive them," and once with a question, "Why have you forsaken me?" Jesus took all the hatred and sin of that day to His grave. He never retaliated. He never defended Himself. He never resisted. Where did all that energy go?

The cosmic singularity of this moment is hard to grasp. Jesus absorbed all the sin that was directed at Him and then converted that energy to love. In Romans 5:7 (NRSV), Paul says, "Rarely will anyone die for a righteous person—though perhaps for a good person someone might actually dare to die. But God proves his love for us in that while we still were sinners Christ died for us." No one had ever done that before. It isn't natural or possible to do so willingly as a human being. Jesus didn't deflect or redirect the sin. He converted the energy of sin to love and transferred love, rather than sin, to others. Such a feat is supernatural. It is divine. No human could endure all that hatred and not sin in return. In Jesus's death, sin didn't defeat Him—Jesus defeated sin.

So 2,000 years later, *how* does the historical day of Good Friday make a person godly? On the cross, Jesus unleashed a love so pure and so strong, the likes of which the world had never seen before. But the world *has* seen this love since then. Starting with Jesus's act of perfect love, individual people have continued to pass on this divine, forgiving, transformative love, person to person, moment by moment, every day since the first Easter when Jesus rose from the dead. This pure love, expressed first by Jesus, turns a heart brutalized by hatred into a heart that responds in love. Stronger than the energy of hate, this love is the only force that stops the ripple effect of sin and evil. Evil spreads person to person, moment by moment like a hidden virus. And like a healing medicine, the grace of Jesus heals person to person, moment by moment when we, like John Perkins, experience the love of Jesus and the forgiveness of our own sins.

WEEKEND READING AND REFLECTION FIVE

☩ **Read Mark 15:1–39**

In this passage there are two levels of authority: (1) the chief priests who were the religious authorities accusing Jesus of blasphemy and deception because He claimed to be the Son of God, and (2) Pontius Pilate, the Roman ruler of the region who charges Jesus with nothing, but nonetheless orders Him to be executed.

1. Pilate has a choice to release _____ or _____. What has each done to be on trial? (Mark 15:6–9) _____

    Why does Pilate think the chief priests handed Jesus over to be crucified? (Mark 15:10) _____

2. Who incites the crowd? (Mark 15:11) _____
    What does the crowd shout? (Mark 15:13–14) _____

3. Who carries Jesus's cross? (Mark 15:21) _____
    What does the inscription of the charge say? (Mark 15:26) _____

4. What words do those passing by use to mock Jesus? (Mark 15:29–32)

5. How long is Jesus on the cross before He dies? (Mark 15:33–34) _____

6. Jesus cries out, "_____ God, _____ God, why _____?" (Mark 15:34). What might this question show us about Jesus's relationship with God?

7. In this chapter, many people watch the crucifixion of Jesus and view it as evidence that He must not be the Messiah, the promised one who will be king. Who watches Jesus die and has a different reaction? (Mark 15:39)

    Why do you think he has a different reaction?

8. What could Jesus have said at His trial to avoid crucifixion? Why would he not say this?

📖 **Read Luke 23:34**

9. What does Jesus pray for the ones who are mocking and killing Him?

Human beings have a cognitive cycle in which stressors that come into the body must have a place to go. We complete the stress cycle by exporting that energy, either in unhealthy or healthy ways. If we don't export the stress, it stays in our bodies and diminishes our well-being. The law of conservation of energy states that energy is neither created nor destroyed; the same applies to our emotional energy and stress. They don't just disappear, but they can change from one energy form to another.

What Jesus did on the cross doesn't violate the law of thermodynamics. When He became fully human, He willingly humbled Himself to live within the natural laws. He didn't eliminate the mockery, hatred, and torture He experienced on the cross. He didn't make it disappear; He converted it. What entered Him was sin and hatred; what came out was love. What came out was divine power—the power of perfect love.

10. Look at the drawing below: Draw additional arrows coming into Jesus, and for each one write words that describe what He experienced. Now look at the arrow coming out of Him, and write what Jesus expressed to God the Father and the crowd.

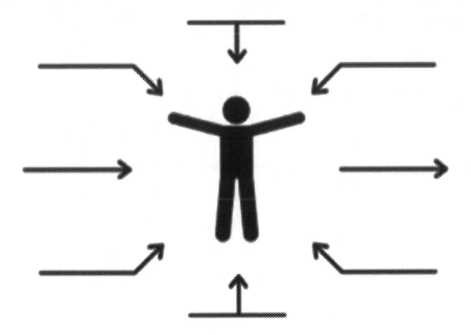

Here are some words you might want to write on the arrows coming in to Jesus: spitting, crown of thorns, flogging, stripping of clothes, mocking salute, taunting, mocking kneeling, nails, shouting, asking "why have you forsaken me?"

Read Luke 23:50–56, 24:1–12
For Jews, the Sabbath is the first day of the week, not the last day.

11. How are the two men dressed who visit the women? (Luke 24:4) Where do they say Jesus is? (Luke 24:5–6)

12. What do the women do with this information? (Luke 24:9) _____
How do the disciples respond? (Luke 24:11)

At the scene of the tomb, the angels appear to three women whose testimony as females isn't valid in court. It is no accident that God uses the words of those who are culturally devalued to bring the truth of the risen Christ. Blindness to see and receive the testimony of those with the least power directly diminishes our capacity to recognize the Kingdom of God unfolding before us.

13. When Peter arrives at the tomb, why do you think his first reaction is amazement instead of the more logical conclusion that the body was stolen? Does the text hint about the reason? (Luke 24:12)

Fast Forward to 1 Peter 4:8 (NIV): "Above all, love each other deeply, because love covers over a multitude of sins." How does Peter experience this deep love from Jesus? How did this love impact John Perkins? What would have happened if Perkins hadn't loved his jailers?

About Affluence in the Kingdom of God

In this passage, Joseph, a wealthy man from Arimathea, takes the body of Jesus, wraps it in linens, and lays it in a tomb. Rather than considering himself above such tasks, he puts his own body in physical contact with the dead, making him unclean according to Jewish law. To be unclean lowers his status in the community. This small vignette in the book of Luke provides a subtle truth for those who are wealthy, not just in money but in resources, power, and abilities. When we participate in lowly and humbling bodily tasks in the service of others, we touch the body of Christ.

In the Parable of the Sower, found in Matthew 13:1–9, Jesus warns about the deceitfulness of riches. How does money deceive us? In what way does it lie? How does it make promises it can't keep? Wealth offers security, beauty, and significance, but does it deliver? People with power, money, and position *look* more secure and happy, but are they? Paradoxically, the Bible teaches that blessing comes to those who are poor in spirit. It is there that we find Christ. In relationships with those in lowly places, the veil is lifted, and we understand that we are the same in our shared humanity. We *become* poor in spirit because we see that we, in fact, *are* poor in spirit. Without God, without a life of meaning, and without love for others, we find ourselves empty and lost no matter how much power, beauty, and success we have.

One Step: Is there someone you need to forgive?

Forgiveness is a journey with many stations. The first step is a choice, not a feeling. Like boarding a train, we choose to step on board and ask God to take us where we need to go. We don't know how long it will take, but the first step is asking God to help us forgive.

This week, we step out of our familiar boat of unforgiveness, either to forgive ourselves or forgive another. This week, I invite you to say these prayers out loud. With this kind of work, it is important to hear your own voice asking for help, instead of praying silently in your mind.

1. Lord, who do I need to forgive today?

   _____

2. Lord, I forgive _____.

3. I can't forgive _____
   Lord, will you help me?

Living an upwardly mobile and comfortable life brings advantages, but it comes with a cost. We aren't in daily relationships with the people who have the most to teach us. Take, for example, my friend Eleanor. In 2020, she suffered a massive stroke that landed her in a rehabilitation center for six months. The cross-cultural friendships she formed during rehab brought her as much healing as the physical therapy she received. Although outwardly her body remains limited, inwardly she experiences a renewed outlook that blesses everyone who knows her. She received the gift of care and became friends with women she never would have met otherwise. As we will see in future lessons, God calls and empowers Peter to traverse cultural divides.

Reader: Hello, and welcome! I hope you all had a good week. For today's reading, I invite you settle into a moment of quiet while I read Mark 16:1–8. Listen for a word or phrase that stands out to you.

Mark 16:1–8 (NIV)

When the Sabbath was over, Mary Magdalene, Mary the mother of James, and Salome bought spices so that they might go to anoint Jesus's body. [2] Very early on the first day of the week, just after sunrise, they were on their way to the tomb [3] and they asked each other, "Who will roll the stone away from the entrance of the tomb?"

[4] But when they looked up, they saw that the stone, which was very large, had been rolled away. [5] As they entered the tomb, they saw a young man dressed in a white robe sitting on the right side, and they were alarmed.

[6] "Don't be alarmed," he said. "You are looking for Jesus the Nazarene, who was crucified. He has risen! He is not here. See the place where they laid him. [7] But go, tell his disciples and Peter, 'He is going ahead of you into Galilee. There you will see him, just as he told you.'"

[8] Trembling and bewildered, the women went out and fled from the tomb. They said nothing to anyone, because they were afraid.

Write the image, word, or phrase that stands out to you: _____

Teaching or Testimony

(o p t i o n a l)

Notes:

1. Does anyone want to share the word, phrase, or image they wrote down during the reading?

2. Review two to three questions in the **Weekend Reading and Reflection** from this week that group members found interesting or important.

3. What is herd mentality? Why do you think the crowd has power over Peter in the courtyard but not in the garden? In what way is the power of belonging a good thing for us as human beings? In what way is it a harmful thing?

4. What is the first law of thermodynamics? Do you see this law at work when you have a stressful day? What are some of the healthy and unhealthy things we do with that stressful energy?

5. Hebrews 12:2 (NRSV) says, "Jesus the pioneer and perfecter of our faith, who for the sake of the joy that was set before him endured the cross, disregarding its shame, and has taken his seat at the right hand of the throne of God." Take a moment to consider the joy that was set before Jesus. What is that joy? What impression does that make on you?

6. Review the **One Step** for the week. How did it go? Do any of you want to share a story of God *lifting* you as you stepped out in faith?

WHAT IS GRACE?

WEEK SIX

At a party one night, I committed the cardinal relationship sin—I criticized my husband in public. While the critiscism wasn't ideal, the real problem was that I said it in front of others. Few things hurt more than when your partner turns on you in front of your friends. Even as the words came out of my mouth, I wanted to take them back. But I didn't, and the damage was done. His face communicated what I knew he was thinking (*I can't believe what you just said to me*).

The next morning, I felt terrible. How could I have talked to him that way in front of everyone? I tried to move on, but guilt nags, and it interfered with my attempt to have a happy and productive day. At the kitchen sink, I thought about what I said as I washed dishes and watched the water flow in and around my fingers while scrubbing pots. I considered how this grievance I committed is a small, personal taste of a larger, human problem. No amount of kindness can undo a wrong committed. No contrite behavior can lift the feeling of guilt. We can apologize, but we can't reverse time or nullify the damage that is done.

That night after the kids went to bed, Steve and I sank into the blue lounge chairs in our kitchen, the ones we added for comfort in a room of hard surfaces. Rather than give me the cold shoulder, he listened as I apologized for my remarks at the party. I told him how I was ashamed that I am the kind of person that I am. Like my mom, I do and say dumb things. I wish I didn't, but I do. She unintentionally embarrassed me growing up, and now I find myself doing the same to my family. Even when I try, sometimes *I do what I do not want to do.*

His reply surprised me. "We all say dumb things that we regret. Don't be so hard on yourself," he said.

He responded not with anger (which I deserved) but with encouragement. I received exactly what I didn't expect but what I needed the most. He didn't wish I would change or fix this part of myself. He didn't minimize and pretend like it didn't bother him either. Instead, he put it in perspective. He made a joke, teased me for being so free-spirited, and then told me to "shake it off." In his unique, unsentimental, Steve-like way, he forgave me and told me not to worry about it. I felt loved inspite of myself. In short, he showed me grace.

How he responded isn't natural. Instinctively, when someone hurts you, you want to hurt that person back. But he did the opposite. His words erased the weight of my regret, and the guilt lifted. He helped me see myself the way he sees me.

My husband absorbed the hurt rather than put it back on me. But there was more. His choice allowed for what I think of as the *jujitsu of redemption*. In jujitsu, you use the force of the opponent's blow against him or her. The harder the opponent hits, the more force you channel to fight back. The same thing happens with redemption. First, forgiveness absorbs the blow. But then, with a jujitsu move, redemption converts the wrong committed into something good. Because of the way my husband responded, this incident that should have harmed our relationship strengthened it instead. Steve's reaction to my failing enlarged my affection for him, more than if I'd never wronged him. His words made me value him above all others, not only because he is my husband but because that kind of love—the kind that loves me at my worst—is better than anything in this world. That is redemption. In scripture we see this jujitsu of redemption repeatedly. What the devil intends for evil, God can use for good.

At its best, marriage is an echo. My husband's love reverberated back to the kind of love that Jesus demonstrates on the cross. When we experience His love, our forgiven sins strengthen our love for God and in turn, give us compassion for others.

Let's watch a moment of redemption in Peter's life when Jesus forgives him and welcomes him back as a friend and disciple.

WEEKEND READING AND REFLECTION SIX

Read about Peter's reinstatement in John 21:4–14.

1. List some aspects of Peter's personality that you see in this story.

2. Where have you seen these personality traits show up before? How is this time different than last time, when Peter got out of the boat?

3. List the miraculous and ordinary things Jesus does to help the disciples recognize Him.

   Thank Jesus for the ordinary and miraculous ways He has been with you recently. List any examples you can think of below.

4. When Jesus asks Peter three times if he loves Him, it hurts Peter. Why do you think he is hurt? Why do you think Jesus asks three times?

5. At the Last Supper, Peter has an inflated view of himself and his ability to follow Jesus, even to the point of death. How could Peter's failure then help him become the kind of person on whom Jesus could build the church?

Jesus's interaction with Peter on the beach, like my conversation with Steve, is a picture of *redemption*. The root word *redeem* means "to buy back." Rather than living with the weight of that guilt, Peter receives Jesus's forgiveness, but that is not all. Jesus buys back Peter's life and gives him a new purpose. Under the grace of Jesus's forgiveness, the shortcomings that mark Peter—his impulsiveness and misguided passion—don't define him. Those personality traits are redeemed for good. For example, this time Peter doesn't step out of the boat; he leaps out of the boat to touch Jesus. He no longer has one foot trusting what this world has to offer and the other foot trusting Jesus. He is *all in*. His passion and pride no longer toss him about like the waves in the sea. He is bold; he has been redeemed.

6. Peter doesn't hide in shame but leaps out of the boat. What does that say about the nature of Jesus's love? How does that moment affect how we approach God when we feel ashamed?

7. Read and write down Hebrews 4:16.

Fast Forward to 1 Peter 2:24 (NRSV). Later in his life Peter writes this to the church: "He [Jesus] himself bore our sins in his body on the cross, so that, free from sins, we might live for righteousness; by his wounds you have been healed." For Peter, how do Jesus's wounds bring healing?

⊞ **Read Acts 1:3–12**

8. What do the disciples expect when they ask Jesus if this is "the time" in verse 6?

9. What does Jesus say that is not for the disciples to know? _____
    Why is it so important to us to know *when*?

10. What does Jesus promise his disciples instead of telling them *when*?

11. What does Jesus want His disciples to be, and where does He want them to go?

The Church refers to this moment in Acts as the Ascension. Ilia Delio, a professor of faith and science at Villanova University, writes this about the Ascension:

> To ascend with Christ does not mean we are to "go up" but to "go down" into the depths of our lives, to live from a center of humility, to accept the truth of each moment gifted by the power of God's love. To think of "what is above," of what is heavenly, is to think out of a deeper center of consciousness, not a consciousness of the isolated self but a consciousness of deep interconnectedness, and to realize that heaven begins here on earth when we realize that we are bound together in the unity of God's ever-flowing love. To attain this unity in love amidst the chaos of world is to ascend with Christ.[14]

One Step: Each day, find one way you can "ascend" with Christ. Brainstorm about what those ways might be.

Reader: Hello, and welcome! I hope you all had a good week. For today's reading, I invite you to settle into a moment of quiet while I read John 21:4–14. Listen for a word or phrase that stands out to you.

John 21:4–14 (NIV)

[4] Early in the morning, Jesus stood on the shore, but the disciples did not realize that it was Jesus.

[5] He called out to them, "Friends, haven't you any fish?"

"No," they answered.

[6] He said, "Throw your net on the right side of the boat and you will find some." When they did, they were unable to haul the net in because of the large number of fish.

[7] Then the disciple whom Jesus loved said to Peter, "It is the Lord!" As soon as Simon Peter heard him say, "It is the Lord," he wrapped his outer garment around him (for he had taken it off) and jumped into the water. [8] The other disciples followed in the boat, towing the net full of fish, for they were not far from shore, about a hundred yards. [9] When they landed, they saw a fire of burning coals there with fish on it, and some bread.

[10] Jesus said to them, "Bring some of the fish you have just caught." [11] So Simon Peter climbed back into the boat and dragged the net ashore. It was full of large fish, but even with so many the net was not torn. [12] Jesus said to them, "Come and have breakfast." None of the disciples dared ask him,

"Who are you?" They knew it was the Lord. [13] Jesus came, took the bread and gave it to them, and did the same with the fish. [14] This was now the third time Jesus appeared to his disciples after he was raised from the dead.

Write the image, word, or phrase that stands out to you: _____

Teaching or Testimony
(optional)

Notes:

SMALL GROUP
DISCUSSION SIX

1. Does anyone want to share the word, phrase, or image they wrote down during the reading?

2. How would you explain the jujitsu of redemption? How does *redeeming love* impact Peter in this story? Why doesn't it impact Judas who, we learn from Scripture (Matthew 27:5), hangs himself after betraying Jesus?

3. How does our culture respond to weakness? In 2 Corinthians 12:9 (NIV), God says, "My grace is sufficient for you, for my power is made perfect in weakness." Have you ever found this verse to be true? If so, how?

4. Hebrews 4:16 (NRSV) says, "Let us therefore approach the throne of grace with boldness, so that we may receive mercy and find grace to help in time of need." What do you think this means, and how does it challenge you today?

5. Reread the quotation by Ilia Delio from this week's lesson. What do you think it means to participate in the ascension of Christ by going "down"?

6. Review the **One Step** for the week. How did it go? What did it look like to "ascend" with Christ by descending?

Lifted by Love • Lessons from the Life of Peter

WHO AM I?

WEEK SEVEN

How do you find proof for the existence of the Holy Spirit, the third person of the Trinity? In a courtroom, lawyers use testimonies as evidence to prove their case. On the stand, a person recounts what he or she experienced firsthand. One eyewitness's testimony doesn't win an argument, but the story plays an important role in building a case. The same holds true in building a case for the Holy Spirit. You can't prove the Holy Spirit with physical evidence, but you can see the effects of the Holy Spirit in many testimonies throughout history. Here is one from my own life.

At a picnic table in July, I sat with my best friends from youth group during family camp. We chewed gum from our Blow Pops and chatted while we waited for our parents to to finish their meeting. On this evening, we decided to play basketball with the other 6th grade boys on the court nearby. It was a way to hang out with boys without the awkwardness of talking to them, which is no small feat for middle school girls. About fifteen minutes into the game, two boys, Jonathan and Andy, accidentally collided on the court. When they fell to the ground, we heard a loud crack and then a scream. I looked over and saw a jarring sight. Andy's right forearm rested at a sharp angle by his side. Clearly, the bone was broken in two.

It only took ten minutes for the ambulance to arrive, but in that time span, many of us started to cry. Listening to Andy's screams over and over broke the shell of safety and innocence that, up until then, was the only reality we knew. The adults nearby busied themselves with the medics, and we were left alone. We wandered outside to a grassy field and sat huddled together. The girls were crying, and the boys were trying not to. I don't know who spoke first, but someone said a prayer. Soon others joined in, one after another, praying small, quiet prayers for Andy. Unlike at meals or bedtimes, no adult prompted us to pray; the words came from a different place than our taught prayers or Sunday school practices. Unscripted, awkward, and vulnerable, we prayed from our hearts.

In the sky above the field where we sat, the sun began to set. Streaks of pink and bright orange appeared on the horizon. The warm summer breezes blew, and we sat together for what seemed like a very long time. Strangely, the praying led to more tears—tears of release and sadness. We cried not just for Andy but for sorrows we never knew we carried. From someplace inside of me, a calm peace emerged, and I knew that no matter what happened, all would be well.

Something unusual happened that night. Christians call that presence the Holy Spirit. At the time, I simply called it God. I look back on that night and know in my heart, in a way that no one can ever take away, that the existence of the Holy Spirit is real, not because I can see or touch that Spirit but because I can feel the Spirit in me and in those around me. This is my testimony. That summer, the experience of God's holy presence was not an illusion. It was not a warm feeling from being with friends after a traumatic incident. That night, I knew what the apostle Paul describes as a love that surpasses understanding. A dozen children on the verge of adulthood sat together and shared a fullness none of us had ever known before.

How do you know the Holy Spirit is real if you can't see or touch the Spirit? The disciple John writes, "The wind blows wherever it pleases. You hear its sound, but you cannot tell where it comes from or where it is going. So it is with everyone born of the Spirit" (John 3:8 NIV). Replicating the experience I had that summer isn't possible, just as determining the direction of the wind isn't feasible. God reveals Himself to all of us in different ways but Scripture is clear: "Ask and it will be given to you; seek and you will find; knock and the door willl be opened to you" (NIV). If we want the Holy Spirit in our lives, we can ask.

While recovering from a stem cell transplant for leukemia, my friend Mary Brooks took short walks in the park near her hospital. Having quarantined in the cancer ward for weeks, the touch of the breeze on her cheeks brought her to tears. She noticed and appreciated the wind like never before.

Now, nearly two years later, she looks for wind. She sees it in ways she never did before. Whenever the leaves rustle in a gentle breeze or the branches bend in the gusts of a storm, she is reminded of God's sustaining presence during that difficult time. Similarly, once you believe in the Holy Spirit, the third person of the Trinity no longer holds an unfamiliar mystique any more than the wind does. You notice the gentle breezes you never paid attention to before. You realize the wind has been there all along, only now you are aware of it.

WEEKEND READING AND REFLECTION SEVEN

Last week we read about Jesus's resurrection and Peter's reinstatement as a disciple. Peter receives Jesus's forgiveness, and it changes him forever. In this next lesson, I invite you to notice the difference this grace makes in Peter's personality.

Read Acts 2:1–8

1. What happens in these verses that astounds the people?

2. What does the first act of the Holy Spirit at Pentecost make possible?

Pentecost is a Jewish holiday that occurs fifty days after Passover. It commemorates when Moses climbed Mount Sinai and received God's law in the form of the Ten Commandments. That law instructs the Israelites how God wants them to live as His people. Here is the account in Exodus 19: 16–19 (NIV):

> On the morning of the third day there was thunder and lightning, with a thick cloud over the mountain, and a very loud trumpet blast. Everyone in the camp trembled. Then Moses led the people out of the camp to meet with God, and they stood at the foot of the mountain. Mount Sinai was covered with smoke, because the LORD descended on it in fire. The smoke billowed up from it like smoke from a furnace, and the whole mountain trembled violently. As the sound of the trumpet grew louder and louder, Moses spoke and the voice of God answered him.

3. What are the similarities between what happens at Mount Sinai and what happens in Acts at Pentecost?

After God comes down from Mount Sinai, He gives Moses the Ten Commandments and writes them on stone tablets. These laws not only teach the Israelite people how to live in a way that honors God but describe how human beings should behave toward on another for the greater good of society. He forms a covenant with His people and tells them, "If you obey me fully and keep my covenant, then out of all nations you will be my treasured possession. Although the whole earth is mine, you will be for me a kingdom of priests and a holy nation" (Exodus 19:5 NIV).

In Acts 2, however, a momentous shift occurs with the covenant formed on Mount Sinai. After Pentecost in Acts, the Holy Spirit is God's empowering presence in our lives so we can live as God's people in His new Kingdom. In Hebrews 10:16–17 (NIV), we learn what has changed: "'This is the covenant I will make with them after that time, says the Lord. I will put my laws in their hearts, and I will write them on their minds.' Then he adds: 'Their sins and lawless acts I will remember no more.' And where these have been forgiven, sacrifice for sin is no longer necessary." God's instruction is no longer ten commandments written on stone tablets. Instead, His ways are impressed on our hearts through the Holy Spirit.

4. Why is "sacrifice for sin" no longer necessary, according to Hebrews 10:17?

📖 **Reread Mark 1:8, a verse from Week 1**

5. Do you think Jesus fulfills the prediction that John the baptizer makes? If so, how is that so since Jesus ascends to heaven in Acts 1?

📖 **Read John 16:5–16.** These words are a part of Jesus's farewell discourse with the disciples.

6. List five things that the Holy Spirit will do.

    (1)

    (2)

    (3)

    (4)

    (5)

7. How does Jesus describe the way the Father, the Son, and the Holy Spirit relate to each other in John 16:15? How does He promise to include us?

Is the Holy Spirit incompatible with science? Richard Rohr, an American Franciscan priest, writes about this topic on his blog. Here is an excerpt.

Perhaps the term "quantum entanglement" names something that we have long intuited, but science has only recently observed. Here is the principle in everyday language: *in the world of quantum physics, it appears that one particle of any entangled pair "knows" what is happening to another paired particle—even though there is no known means for such information to be communicated between the particles, which are separated by sometimes very large distances.*

Scientists don't know how far this phenomenon applies beyond very rare particles, but quantum entanglement hints at a universe where everything is in relationship, in communion, and also where that communion can be resisted ("sin"). Both negative and positive entanglement in the universe matter, maybe even ultimately matter. Prayer, intercession, healing, love and hate, heaven and hell, all make sense on a whole new level. Almost all religions have long pointed to this entanglement. In Paul's letter to the Romans (14:7) he says quite clearly "the life and death of each of us has its influence on others." The Apostles' Creed states that we believe in "the communion of saints." There is apparently a positive inner connectedness that we can draw upon if we wish.

Ilia Delio says, "If reality is nonlocal, that is, if things can affect one another despite distance or space-time coordinates, then nature is not composed of material substances but deeply entangled fields of energy; the nature of the universe is undivided wholeness." I've often described this phenomenon as an experiential "force field" or the Holy Spirit. In Trinitarian theology, the Holy Spirit is foundationally described as the *field of love* between the Father and the Son. One stays in this positive force field whenever one loves, cares, or serves with positive energy. I know that when people stand in this place, when they rest in love as their home base, they become quite usable by God, and their lives are filled with "quantum entanglements" that result in very real healings, forgiveness, answered prayers, and new freedom for those whom they include in the force field with them. I have too many examples here to list or to even remember. Jung called these events "synchronicities"; secular folks call them coincidences; the Sisters of Charity of Leavenworth, who taught me, called them Divine Providence.

On the other end of the spectrum there are people who carry death wherever they go, toward all those they can pull into their negative force field. (Is this hell?) I know that when I regress into any kind of intentional negativity toward anything or anybody, even in my mind, I am actually hurting and harming them. Etty Hillesum, a young, imprisoned Jew in Nazi-occupied Amsterdam, says straightforwardly, "Each of us moves things along in the direction of war every time we fail to love." And if so, it would surely follow that each of us moves things along in the direction of healing each time we *choose* to love. Each time it is a conscious choice and a decision, at least to some degree. Grace and guilt both glide on such waves of desire and intention.

Consciousness, desire, and intentionality matter. Maybe they even create and destroy worlds. We cannot afford to harbor hate or hurt or negativity in any form. We must deliberately choose to be instruments of peace—first of all in our minds and hearts. Such daring simplicity is *quantum entanglement* with the life and death of all things. We largely create both heaven and hell. God is not "in" heaven nearly as much as God is the force field that allows us to create heaven through our intentions and actions. Once quantumly entangled, it seems we are entangled forever, which is why we gave such finality and urgency to our choices for life (heaven) or death (hell).[15]

8. We can't see the Holy Spirit, but like the wind, we see where it is moving. We can experience its effect on the world. Do you see evidence of the Holy Spirit either in your life or in the world around you? If so, how?

📖 **Read Acts 3:1–16**

Christians believe that Jesus is the *incarnation* of God. The Latin root word is *caro,* which means "flesh." Therefore, Jesus is God embodied in flesh. He lived in a specific time in history. In contrast, the Holy Spirit in not physical matter and not bound by time or space.

9. By what power does Peter heal the beggar? (Acts 3:6) _____
   What kind of place in society would a man have who was crippled from birth?

10. In Acts 3:12, Peter denies any _____ or _____ of his own in performing the miracle.

11. For those who have been practicing our faith for years, in what way might we put our faith in piety, or religious living? What effect does this have on us and those around us?

12. How has reliance on the Holy Spirit's power changed Peter?

📖 **Read Acts 4:1–22**

13. Who arrests Peter and John, and why? (Acts 4:1–3)

14. What enables Peter to speak boldly? (Acts 4:8)

15. Why are the religious leaders amazed? (Acts 4:13)

16. How do Peter and John respond to the orders not to speak or teach in the name of Jesus? Why do you think Peter no longer denies Jesus when he is threatened by authorities?

Fast Forward to 2 Peter 1:3-4 (NIV). Peter writes to the early Church, "His divine power has given us everything we need for a godly life through our knowledge of him who called us by his own glory and goodness. Through these he has given us his very great and precious promises, so that through them you may participate in the *divine nature*, having escaped the corruption in the world caused by evil desires" (emphasis added). What do you think Peter means by the divine nature? How would you describe it as you see it in Peter?

One Step: Every country has a culture. The "divine nature" Peter refers to in his letter describes the culture of the Kingdom of God on earth. We need the empowering love of the Holy Spirit to help us participate in the divine nature of love. We can't do it with our own natural love. What is one specific way you can ask the Holy Spirit to empower you to live the divine nature of love this week? Write that one-step prayer here.

Reader: Hello, and welcome! I hope you all had a good week. For today's reading, I invite you to settle into a moment of quiet while I read Acts 3:1–10. Listen for a word or phrase that stands out to you.

Acts 3:1–10 (NIV)

Peter Heals a Lame Beggar

One day Peter and John were going up to the temple at the time of prayer—at three in the afternoon. [2] Now a man who was lame from birth was being carried to the temple gate called Beautiful, where he was put every day to beg from those going into the temple courts. [3] When he saw Peter and John about to enter, he asked them for money. [4] Peter looked straight at him, as did John. Then Peter said, "Look at us!" [5] So the man gave them his attention, expecting to get something from them.

[6] Then Peter said, "Silver or gold I do not have, but what I do have I give you. In the name of Jesus Christ of Nazareth, walk." [7] Taking him by the right hand, he helped him up, and instantly the man's feet and ankles became strong. [8] He jumped to his feet and began to walk. Then he went with them into the temple courts, walking and jumping, and praising God. [9] When all the people saw him walking and praising God, [10] they recognized him as the same man who used to sit begging at the temple gate called Beautiful, and they were filled with wonder and amazement at what had happened to him.

Write the image, word, or phrase that stands out to you: _____

Teaching or Testimony

(o p t i o n a l)

Notes:

SMALL GROUP
DISCUSSION SEVEN

1. Does anyone want to share the word, phrase, or image they wrote down during the reading?

2. Review one or two questions in the **Weekend Reading and Reflection** from this week that group members found interesting or important.

3. The *Life with God Bible* includes the observation that in Acts, we see the clash between "kingdomless power" and "powerless kingdoms." What is the difference?[16] How do we see both types in the reading for this week? Can anyone read a particular verse that demonstrates either "kingdomless power" or "powerless kingdoms"?

4. Striking parallels exist between the Passover in the Old Testament and the Passover meal at the Last Supper in the New Testament. With what you've learned so far, what is the story of the first Passover in the Old Testament, and how does Jesus's death and resurrection add new meaning to that story? (See note on Passover in Week 4 or refer to Exodus 12.)

5. As we near the end of this study, let's look back and reflect on how Peter changes. As a group, let's see what we can remember. Brainstorm and write down the stories you recall that reveal the old versus the new character traits of Peter.

Character Traits Old vs. New	Story of Old Peter	Story of New Peter
Expectations *of* Jesus vs. Hope *in* Jesus	Peter corrects Jesus for predicting His death because Peter expects Him to be the new earthly king.	Jesus has already died and risen. Peter spreads Jesus's message to others even though he knows Jesus's Kingdom is in the heart, not on the throne in Rome.
Ambition for Himself vs. Ambition for the mission of Jesus		
Fear vs. Trust		
Inflated view of himself vs. Limitless confidence in Jesus's Spirit		
Ashamed of Jesus vs. Unashamed of Jesus		
Impulsive and passionate vs. Bold and fearless		

6. Review the **One Step** for the week. How did it go? Do any of you want to share a story of God helping you participate in His divine nature?

Lifted by Love • Lessons from the Life of Peter

WHERE AM I GOING?

WEEK EIGHT

On April 3, 1968, the day before he was assassinated in Memphis, Tennessee, Dr. Martin Luther King, Jr. decided *not* to give a Sunday sermon. He wasn't feeling well, so he asked his best friend, Ralph Abernathy, to preach on his behalf. Once inside the sanctuary, however, Abernathy called King and told him to come to the church. He felt that King should be there even if he only shared a few words after the sermon. King agreed. While listening to Ralph Abernathy preach, King was stirred by the Holy Spirit to get up and preach after him. What followed was one of the most memorable speeches of all time. If you listen to the cadence of his voice on a recording, the final words end as if he is mid-sentence, as if there is more to come. Benjamin Hooks remembers this about that night: "When he [King] finished, he stopped by quoting the words of that song that he loved so well, 'Mine eyes have seen the glory of the coming of the Lord.' He never finished. He wheeled around and took his seat and to my surprise, when I got a little closer, I saw tears streaming down his face. Grown men were sitting there weeping openly because of the power of this man who spoke on that night."[17]

What is the difference between hope and wishful thinking? Dr. King's hope for the future is more than a wish or longing. It is a vision. In the following words from the end of his speech, imagine that you hear his voice—triumphant, lyrical, and with poignant pauses when applause breaks through. You will hear how his hope is more than a wish; his hope calls people to action.

> We've got some difficult days ahead. But it really doesn't matter with me now. Because I've been to the mountaintop. [applause] And I don't mind. Like anybody, I would like to live a long life. Longevity has its place. But I'm not concerned about that now. I just want to do God's will. And He's allowed me to go up to the mountain. And I've looked over. And I've seen the promised land. I may not get there with you. But I want you to know tonight, that we, as a people, will get to the promised land! So I'm happy tonight. I'm not worried about anything. I'm not fearing any man. Mine eyes have seen the glory of the coming of the Lord![18]

By the power of the Holy Spirit, Dr. King glimpses the glory of the coming of the Lord. Death threats mount, but his eyes are fixed on the Promised Land. He isn't worried about anything. He doesn't fear any man. His hope is fixed, his faith steadfast, and his love unwavering. On the last night of his life, in his weeping, he experiences the glory of God's Kingdom on earth. The future hope breaks into the present, and he is filled with the fullness of God.

Dr. King's life would soon come to an end, but the promise of his hope tells a different story. No circumstances, no plot against him, no anti-Civil Rights Movement can dim his vision of the future. He sees the glory of the Lord. He sees the Promised Land. Like a fishing line cast into the future, Dr. King's hope hooks onto heaven and reels it into the present. His hope in God pulls the *then* toward the *now*. Biblical hope isn't a wishful thought; it has substance. It changes the present because it changes *how* we live in the present.

How does that work? Imagine that Dr. King only *wishes* for a better world without any certainty of what will come. Imagine how discouraging the Civil Rights Movement must have been during the long marches, protests, setbacks, and imprisonments. What enables him to uphold his convictions of non-violence in the face of such violence? *Hope.* Biblical hope isn't an abstract idea. It is alive. Biblical hope rests on Jesus, not on circumstances. Biblical hope gives us strength when all earthly hope is lost. Biblical hope doesn't die with one gunshot on the balcony of a motel in Memphis. Biblical hope lifts our eyes to what is to come, and by living in that hope, we bring a taste of heaven to earth now.

At the end of his life, Peter wrote, "Praise be to the God and Father of our Lord Jesus Christ! In his great mercy he has given us new birth into a living hope through the resurrection of Jesus Christ from the dead" (1 Peter 1:3 NIV). How is hope *living?* Biblical hope changes how I live *now.*

We live knowing that:

- God is renewing all things (Revelation 21.1–5).
- Light that shines in the darkness will not be overcome (John 1:5).
- Nothing can separate me from the love of God in Christ Jesus (Romans 8:31–39)
- God is bringing His kingdom to earth for all people (Genesis 12:2–3).
- God works all things together for good when we are in His love (Romans 8:28).

The writer of Hebrews says, "Now faith is the assurance of things hoped for, the conviction of things not seen" (Hebrews 11:1 NRSV). Faith in God's promises *gives substance to hope*. Faith puts hands and feet, words and deeds on hope. Faith unpacks the boxes from your future home and sets up shop in your living room. I treat my husband and children differently since I know God loves them and is working in them for their good. I think about my enemies differently since I know God's love extends to all people. I accept my circumstances differently since I know God is in control of the ultimate outcomes of this world. I grieve loss differently since I know that death doesn't have the final word. I have the courage to face my own failures and shortcomings since I know God loves me at my worst. I find the grace to forgive others because I know the depth of my own need for forgiveness. Hope in the risen Christ changes everything.

In our final lesson this week, we see a glimpse of that future take hold on earth. Rome crucified Peter in AD 64 for his faith, but God continues to extend His covenant blessing to more and more people, inviting them to be born into a new way of living, one that is love-centered, not self-centered. This revolutionary love undergirds every aspect of the Kingdom of God. It not only transforms the individual, like it did Peter, but it transforms the world.

Peter lives out this revolutionary love. He reels the hope of what is to come into the early Church. The Bible calls the first evidence of future glory "firstfruits" of the new kingdom. They are signposts pointing to where we are going. They are a foretaste of what heaven is like. We see glimpses of reconciliation, unity, restoration, and healing. And we, like Peter, live in that same hope and revolutionary love. We participate in bringing this divine nature of God's Kingdom into the world today.

WEEKEND READING AND REFLECTION EIGHT

[†] **Read Acts 10:1–7**

1. What do we know about Cornelius? What do we learn about God in these verses?

[quill icon] In Exodus, God gives the Israelites many laws to show them how to flourish as people. Their way of life sets them apart from the other people who the Jews call Gentiles. Since the Gentiles do not adhere to the Mosaic laws, the Jews consider the Gentiles to be unclean and won't eat with them or go inside their houses. In this week's Scripture text, Cornelius, a Gentile, complicates the typical cultural categories of the day. He worships Israel's God but does not adopt all the Jewish customs such as circumcision, the Sabbath, and ritual cleansing.

[†] **Read Acts 10:9–23**

2. Describe Peter's vision.

3. It is not surprising that Peter's vision is about food since he was hungry. Why is it significant that he has the vision three times?

4. In Acts 10:14, Peter says he has *never* eaten anything impure or unclean. Imagine that you and everyone in your community had never eaten certain foods as an act of obedience to God. What does the voice say in Acts 10:15? Imagine this paradigm shift

for Peter. The text says twice that Peter took time to think and wonder about the vision. What might he have been thinking?

In Genesis 12:1–4, God establishes a covenant with Abraham that He will make him and his descendants into a great nation. God promises that He will bless *all* people on earth *through* Abraham. This pattern of God revealing Himself to a few in order to bless many repeats in this week's text.

Read Acts 10:23–43

5. Who is Peter speaking to in these verses?

6. Before Jesus's death and resurrection, the disciples (including Peter) are concerned with their position of greatness in the new Kingdom of God (Luke 9:46). How has Peter changed? (10:25-26). In what way has Peter's ambition shifted in its end goal and yet remained, but with a new goal?

7. What is the momentous statement Peter makes to Cornelius in Acts 10:28?

8. Referring to Acts 10:34–35, before Peter's vision, how does Peter think God's favor is earned?

9. At this time in history, Jews did not associate with anyone who they considered to be impure or unclean. In this short series of visions, God overturns hundreds of years of separation that occurred between the Israelites and the rest of the world. The dividing wall between them crumbles. What kind of walls (seen and unseen) do we put up to separate us from other people?

10. Sometimes we can identify with the Gentiles. We feel like our lives aren't clean enough for God. Have you ever felt like you needed to make your life more pure before you pray or go to church? According to Acts 10:43, what does our faith rest on in Jesus's new Kingdom? Who makes us clean and earns us our right standing with God? How is that a shift from the old ways?

11. Being friends with someone who is different from you can be difficult, yet God's Spirit instructs and equips Peter to join in fellowship with the Gentiles. What does that say about the new Kingdom?

Caesarea was an important Roman city next to the Mediterranean Sea. It was built by Herod the Great to force all traders to come through the port and pay a tax. Because of that, the city became a place through which people from all over the world traveled. For a group of Gentiles in the town of Caesarea to be given the gift of the Holy Spirit ensured that the news would spread all over the world. In the ancient world, that was like #holyspirit going viral.

Read 1 Corinthians 12: 12–20

12. What is the body of Christ? How is one brought into this body?

13. What do these verses say about belonging? What do they say about our differences? (1 Corinthians 12:15–20)

14. What do these verses say about needing others in areas where we are weak? About helping others in areas where we are strong?

15. What do these verses say about suffering?

16. According to this passage, what is at stake when we spend time wishing we were more like someone else?

Fast Forward to 1 Peter 1:3–4. In the letter Peter writes to the early church, he says this about living hope: "By his great mercy he has given us a new birth into a living hope through the resurrection of Jesus Christ from the dead, and into an inheritance that is imperishable, undefiled, and unfading, kept in heaven for you."

Dr. King envisioned a future where people are united as one in Christ, and so did Peter. What three words does Peter use to describe what we hope for?

_____, _____ and _____

One Step: In the space below, write one area where you can practice living hope this week. What are some ways you plan to do this?

Reader: Hello, and welcome! I hope you all had a good week. For today's reading, I invite you to settle into a moment of quiet while I read 1 Corinthians 13:1–13. Listen for a word or phrase that stands out to you.

1 Corinthians 13:1–13 (NIV)

If I speak in the tongues of men or of angels, but do not have love, I am only a resounding gong or a clanging cymbal. [2] If I have the gift of prophecy and can fathom all mysteries and all knowledge, and if I have a faith that can move mountains, but do not have love, I am nothing. [3] If I give all I possess to the poor and give over my body to hardship that I may boast, but do not have love, I gain nothing.

[4] Love is patient, love is kind. It does not envy, it does not boast, it is not proud. [5] It does not dishonor others, it is not self-seeking, it is not easily angered, it keeps no record of wrongs. [6] Love does not delight in evil but rejoices with the truth. [7] It always protects, always trusts, always hopes, always perseveres.

[8] Love never fails. But where there are prophecies, they will cease; where there are tongues, they will be stilled; where there is knowledge, it will pass away. [9] For we know in part and we prophesy in part, [10] but when completeness comes, what is in part disappears. [11] When I was a child, I talked like a child, I thought like a child, I reasoned like a child. When I became a man, I put the ways of childhood behind me. [12] For now we see only a reflection as in a mirror; then we shall see face to face. Now I know in part; then I shall know fully, even as I am fully known.

¹³ And now these three remain: faith, hope and love. But the greatest of these is love.

Write the image, word, or phrase stands out: _____

Teaching or Testimony
(o p t i o n a l)

Notes:

SMALL GROUP
DISCUSSION EIGHT

1. Does anyone want to share the word, phrase, or image they wrote down during the reading?

2. Review one or two questions in the **Weekend Reading and Reflection** from this week that group members found interesting or important.

3. Review the **One Step** for the week. How did it go? Do any of you want to share a story about living in hope?

4. **Closing Thoughts:** As a group, think back over *Lifted by Love*. What are some of your main takeaways? Here is a recap of each week's topic and text to help you remember:

   1. **Who Is in Charge?**
      Bible stories: John baptizes Jesus. Jesus announces that the Kingdom of heaven is near. Jesus calls His first disciples and fills their nets with fish.

   2. **What Do I Want?**
      Bible stories: Peter declares Jesus is the Son of God. Jesus gives him the name *petra* and says, (Welwood 2022)"on this rock I will build my church." Peter becomes a

stumbling block and misunderstands Jesus's mission to lay down His life. Peter offers to build a structure for Jesus at His transfiguration.

3. **Who Do I Trust?**

   Bible story: Jesus calls Peter to get out of the boat and come to Him.

4. **Am I Good Enough?**

   Bible stories: At the Last Supper, Jesus washes the disciples' feet. Jesus prays for Peter's faith not to fail. Peter betrays Jesus three times.

5. **What is love?**

   Bible stories: Jesus is tried and crucified. Joseph of Arimathea prepares Jesus's body for burial.

6. **What Is Grace?**

   Bible stories: The tomb is empty. Jesus reinstates Peter on the beach. Christ ascends.

7. **Who Am I?**

   Bible stories: The coming of the Holy Spirit at Pentecost. Peter speaks boldly and with authority.

8. **Where Am I Going?**

   Bible stories: Peter dreams about the Gentiles. The Holy Spirit comes to the Gentiles. The body of Christ is made up of many parts and members.

5. Thinking back over the last eight weeks, what is something you are grateful for about this time together?

BIBLIOGRAPHY

@DailyKeller. *Twitter.* 2017.

Delio, Ilia. "A Short Reflection on the Feast of the Ascension." *Center for Christogenesis.* https://christogenesis.org/a-short-reflection-on-the-feast-of-the-ascension/.

"Disciple." *Lexico.* https://www.lexico.com/definition/disciple.

Ellis, Catherine, and Stephen Drury Smith, eds. *Say It Plain: A Century of Great African American Speeches.* (New York: The New Press, 2007).

Fleming, Rutledge. "The Three Hours Devotion." *Saint Thomas Church.* March 30, 2018. https://www.saintthomaschurch.org/events/the-three-hours-devotion-2018-03-30/.

Foster, Richard J., Dallas Willard, Walter Brueggemann, and Eugene H. Peterson. "Acts." *The Life with God Bible.* (San Francisco: Harper San Francisco, 2006).

Greene, Kim, *Wellspring Bible Study, (*West End Presbyterian Church, Richmond, Virginia, 2010).

Hendrickson, William, quoted in "How Jesus Restored Peter." *Keep Believing Ministries.* https://www.keepbelieving.com/how-jesus-restored-peter/.

Hizmi, Hananya. "Archelaus Builds Archelais." *Biblical Archaeology Review* 34, no. 4 (July/August 2008), https://www.baslibrary.org/biblical-archaeology-review/34/4/11.

Hooks, Benjamin, quoted in "Martin Luther King Jr. (1929-1968)." *American Public Media.* http://americanradioworks.publicradio.org/features/sayitplain/mlking.html.

Keller, Timothy. *Counterfeit Gods* (London: Penguin Books, 2009).

Keller, Timothy J. *King's Cross* (London: Hodder & Stoughton, 2011).

"Kingdom of God." *Britannica*. https://www.britannica.com/topic/Kingdom-of-God.

Lewis, C. S. *Mere Christianity* (New York: Macmillan Publishing Company, 1952).

NRSV Bible footnote, Matthew 16:18 (39 in the book of Matthew).

"Perfect." *Lexico*. https://www.lexico.com/en/definition/perfect.

Rohr, Richard. "Quantum Entanglement." *Center for Action and Contemplation* (blog). November 12, 2015. https://cac.org/quantum-entanglement-2015-11-12/.

"The Three Hours Devotion." *Saint Thomas Church*. March 30, 2018. https://www.saintthomaschurch.org/events/the-three-hours-devotion-2018-03-30/.

Welwood, Jennifer. "Unconditional." https://jenniferwelwood.com.

"What's Wrong with the World?" *Chesterton.org*. https://www.chesterton.org/wrong-with-world/.

Wright, N. T. *Lent for Everyone: Mark, Year B: A Daily Devotional*. Google Books.

ENDNOTES

1 "Kingdom of God," *Britannica*, https://www.britannica.com/topic/Kingdom-of-God.

2 Timothy J. Keller, *King's Cross* (London: Hodder & Stoughton, 2011).

3 "What's Wrong with the World?" *Chesterton.org*, https://www.chesterton.org/wrong-with-world/.

4 C. S. Lewis, *Mere Christianity* (New York: Macmillan Publishing Company, 1952), 55–56.

5 "Disciple," *Lexico*, https://www.lexico.com/definition/disciple.

6 NRSV Bible footnote, Matthew 16:18 (39 in the book of Matthew).

7 Timothy J. Keller, *King's Cross* (London: Hodder & Stoughton, 2011).

8 Hananya Hizmi, "Archelaus Builds Archelais," *Biblical Archaeology Review* 34, no. 4 (July/August 2008), https://www.baslibrary.org/biblical-archaeology-review/34/4/11.

9 N. T. Wright, *Lent for Everyone: Mark, Year B: A Daily Devotional*, Google Books, 84.

10 Kim Greene, Wellspring Bible Study, West End Presbyterian Church, Richmond, Virginia, 2010.

11 Ibid.

12 William Hendrickson, quoted in "How Jesus Restored Peter," *Keep Believing Ministries*, https://www.keepbelieving.com/how-jesus-restored-peter/.

13 "The Three Hours Devotion," *Saint Thomas Church*, March 30, 2018, https://www.saintthomaschurch.org/events/the-three-hours-devotion-2018-03-30/.

14 Ilia Delio, "Á Short Reflection on the Feast of the Ascension," *Center for Christogenesis*, https://christogenesis.org/a-short-reflection-on-the-feast-of-the-ascension/.

15 Richard Rohr, "Quantum Entanglement," *Center for Action and Contemplation* (blog), November 12, 2015, https://cac.org/quantum-entanglement-2015-11-12/.

16 Richard J. Foster, Dallas Willard, Walter Brueggemann, and Eugene H. Peterson, "Acts," *The Life with God Bible* (San Francisco: Harper San Francisco, 2006).

17 Benjamin Hooks, quoted in "Martin Luther King Jr. (1929-1968)," *American Public Media*, http://americanradioworks.publicradio.org/features/sayitplain/mlking.html.

18 Ibid.

Printed in the United States
by Baker & Taylor Publisher Services